RESEMBLANCE AND IDENTITY

Panayot Butchvarov

Resemblance and Identity

An Examination
of the Problem of Universals

Indiana University Press / Bloomington & London

Published in Canada by Fitzhenry & Whiteside Limited,
Don Mills, Ontario
Library of Congress catalog card number: 66-22437
ISBN: 0-253-35008-5
Manufactured in the United States of America

*To my father
and to the memory of my mother*

Contents

Preface

The problem of universals has aroused the interest of philosophers probably longer and more consistently than any other philosophical issue. Perhaps this is why the difficulties in discussions of it seem often due to failure to look for and isolate the essential issue in virtue of which it is a separate philosophical problem, and to distinguish it clearly from the many other issues, queries, and difficulties that have accumulated around it in the course of its long history. If the problem of universals is a genuine problem at all, it should be clearly distinguishable from the problems of the nature of knowledge, of thought, of existence, or of meaning. Indeed, its philosophical importance is not limited to its demand for an account of what there is. It is probably true that if there are universals, then our knowledge of their relations would be *a priori*, the possibility of classification would be accounted for, one (but certainly not all) of the necessary conditions of the meaningfulness of general and abstract singular words could be made clear, and at least some contribution would be made to our understanding

of the nature of abstract thinking. But one does not discover that there are universals, nor does one even understand what might be meant by the word "universal," if
one merely argues that synthetic *a priori* knowledge, or
classification, or abstract thinking, or the meaning of
general and abstract singular words can be explained
only by the existence of universals. For the terms "universal," "particular," and "abstract," as employed by
philosophers, are technical terms. Before they are used
for the statement of philosophical theories, the need for
the introduction of such terms must be made clear and
their meaning must be explained. And if they are to
have a distinctive and thus useful, philosophically enlightening, function, they must be carefully distinguished from other, already established, terms, such as
"unobservable entity," "nonspatiotemporal entity," "the
meaning of a word."

It has been argued, for instance, that abstract thought
requires universals for its objects, and that abstract singular words require universals for their referents. As a
matter of historical fact, these arguments have usually
depended on the dubious assumptions, respectively, that
thinking is a kind of contemplation of entities, and that
only linguistic expressions that designate can have meaning. This already suggests that a useful discussion of
such arguments has little to gain from a theory of universals, for it should concern itself mainly with topics
such as the notion of mental entity, the criteria of meaning, and the nature of thought. But even if we could
believe, purely on the basis of considerations concerning
the nature of thought and of language, that there are entities which are special objects of abstract thought and

referents of abstract singular words, we still ought to have *another* reason for classifying such entities as universals. The application of the word "universal" to them, unless it is entirely vacuous, must *add* a new, distinctive element to our description of their nature; it must not be merely another way of saying that these entities are objects of abstract thought and referents of abstract singular words. It may be plausible to suppose that such entities are unobservable, nonspatiotemporal, otherworldly, and rather mysterious. But so far there would be no more reason for classifying them as universals than there would be for classifying God, angels, and disembodied souls as universals. It would be equally useless to appeal to the fact that the kind of thought in question is *abstract* thought and that the linguistic expressions in question are *abstract* singular words. For it is obvious that we describe such thought and such expressions as abstract only because they seem to have as their objects or referents entities which are described, *for independent reasons,* as abstract entities or universals. It is these independent reasons for describing an entity as abstract or as a universal and the exact sense of such a description that constitute a genuine part of the problem of universals. And once these reasons are explained, it may well be found that we have much better grounds for believing that there are universals than the assumptions that thinking is a contemplation of objects and that all meaningful words must have actual referents.

The first task of this essay, therefore, is the development of a distinctive and philosophically useful notion of universal, and of a corresponding statement of the problem of universals as a separate philosophical issue.

Its second task is the solution of the so-stated problem of
universals. Roughly, I shall identify the notion of universal with that of universal quality, in a very wide sense
of the word "quality" to be explained in section 1. And I
shall offer an explanation of the notion of universal
quality that does not depend on the employment of the
technical philosophical terms "universal," "particular,"
or "abstract." I shall identify the problem of universals
with the question whether there are universal qualities,
i.e., whether the qualities of individual things are universal or particular, or, as I shall actually state it without the use of the terms "universal" and "particular,"
whether certain qualities of individual things should be
described as being one and the same quality or distinct
qualities related by a relation of resemblance. Other
questions concerning universals, I believe, are either
consequences or unclear modifications of this primary
problem, or else independent philosophical issues having no special relation to the puzzles concerning universals. That this is so will become evident, I hope, in the
course of our inquiry, especially in sections 1, 2, 5, 13,
17, and 18. But I shall not engage in the historical and
exegetic investigations necessary for an actual proof of
this claim.

My statement of the problem of universals, in particular the identification of the notion of universal with
that of universal quality, accords well with important
traditional conceptions, such as "the universal is common, since that is called universal which is such as to
belong to more than one thing" (Aristotle), and "the
universal is that which is in many and of many" (Albert
the Great). But does it not fail to take account of the

second part of the equally important traditional question "whether genera and species really exist or are bare notions only; and if they exist whether they are corporeal things, or incorporeal and rather separated, or whether they exist in things perceived by the senses and in relation to them," (Porphyry)? For it seems to exclude from consideration one of the major theories of universals: that "genera and species exist not in sensibles but in separation from sensibles," and that universals may exist even if they have no instances. Now if this theory amounts to the claim that qualities, whether particular or universal, need not be qualities *of* individual things, that the notions of genus and species can be explained independently of those of instantiation or participation, then indeed we need not consider it, since, in virtue of the very notions of quality, genus, and species, it is obviously false. But the theory need not be interpreted so crudely as to become obviously false. It can be interpreted as claiming that there is an enormous, categorial difference between individual things and universal qualities and that because of this difference the senses in which universal qualities can be said to exist and to be in space and time, and the senses in which individual things can be said to exist and to be in space and time are so different that one can assert the existence of a quality on the ground that it *can* have instances, even if in fact it has not. I shall consider this claim at the end of the book. But the logically prior questions are, "What is a universal quality?" and "Are there universal qualities?" It is mainly to these questions that I shall address myself in this essay.

In many ways the problem of universals is the paradigm of a philosophical problem. It bears virtually no resemblance to any issue of experimental science. It is supremely general, in the sense that it concerns a certain fact about all qualities, in any actual or possible world, in complete abstraction from circumstances and contexts. And it is neither overtly nor disguisedly a problem *about* philosophy, one which is of interest to philosophers only because of their self-consciousness about the status and possibility of their discipline. Perhaps this is why writers on the problem of universals are especially tempted to connect their inquiries with considerations about philosophical method. I have succumbed to this temptation, mainly in Chapter Three.

In content, if not in style, this essay is intended to be metaphysical. Part of its purpose is to demonstrate, in the context of a specific philosophical topic, that at least one branch of philosophy is a legitimate cognitive discipline that has as its subject matter, not certain features of language or of mathematics, but the essential and most general characteristics of the world.

I wish to express my appreciation to Mr. J. Renford Bambrough, Professor Max Black, and Professor Clyde L. Hardin for their very valuable comments on the manuscript.

P. B.

RESEMBLANCE AND IDENTITY

Introduction

1. The Recurrence of Qualities

In addition to the individual things in the world, such as stones, people, and hats, we distinguish, compare, and claim to have knowledge about their various qualities, properties, characteristics, and relations. I can notice that there is a hat on the rack without noticing its color; but I can also notice the color of the hat and perhaps even ignore the hat itself. I may describe the hat as brown, or as a hat, or as hanging on the rack, and if there are two hats on the rack I may describe them as a pair. But I may also describe the *color* of the hat as darker than the color of the coat which it ought to match, I can assert that the *kind* of thing the hat is serves a purpose somewhat similar to that of shoes, I may know that the hat's *hanging on* the rack is due to my putting it there, and I may point out that the *number* of hats on the rack today is smaller than the number of hats on the rack yesterday.

I shall use the word "quality" as a general term for

any characteristic, relation, or kind of an individual thing or collection of individual things. Thus the color of a hat, its kind or sort, its relation to the rack, and the number of hats on the rack would all be qualities in my sense of this term. The introduction of such a sense of the word "quality" is not intended to suggest that there are not very great differences among such characteristics or features of individual things, which may be of considerable philosophical importance. But, as will become obvious to the reader, nothing in our inquiry will turn on these differences. What I shall have to say will be true, if true at all, of anything that would ordinarily be described as a quality, or characteristic, or relation of an individual thing or collection of individual things. Indeed, I shall use as examples mostly qualities such as colors and shapes. But the only reason for this will be the greater simplicity and familiarity of such examples.

Among the various kinds of fact about qualities of individual things that we generally note and describe, there is one which has seemed especially interesting and important to philosophers. Consider the relationship between the *shape* of one penny and the *shape* of another penny which can be described by saying either (1) that the shape of the one penny resembles (exactly)[1] the shape of the other penny, or (2) that the shape of the one penny and the shape of the other penny are one and the same, or (3) that both the shape of the one penny and the shape of the other penny can be correctly described by the general word "circular." Similar statements can be made

1. Or, is (just) like. The important distinction between exact and inexact resemblance or likeness will be introduced in Chapter Two.

about any two circular things. Thus, however different they may be in other respects, circular things seem to constitute, by their very nature, a distinct group of things. If we know certain truths about the shape of one of them, we seem also to know similar truths about the shapes of all of them without further investigation. Whatever the number and diversity of circular things may be, we are able to consider them as a whole and thus to find a certain unity, simplicity, and intelligibility in what is perhaps an infinite number of very different things. The group of circular things seems to possess a kind of permanence which is completely independent of the existence, location, and the other characteristics and properties of any individual circular thing. And one can inquire into the geometrical characteristics of the shape of a circular thing without paying any attention to the nature or even existence of the thing. Philosophers have been impressed by this seeming importance of the kind of relationship that holds among the shapes of circular things and have constructed elaborate theories to explain its role in knowledge, meaning, and thought. But whether any such theories are justified, and which are justified, cannot be determined properly unless we are clear about the nature of the relationship itself.

The above three statements that describe the relationship between the shapes of two pennies seem to draw attention to one and the same fact, and all three would be considered correct in everyday discourse. Nevertheless, they also appear to be very different. The first statement seems to suggest that the shape of the one penny and the shape of the other penny are distinct qualities which are related by the relation of resemblance. The second statement seems to suggest that, on the contrary, the shape of the one penny is not distinct from the shape of the other penny, that in fact they are one and the same shape, which happens to be the shape of two distinct individual things at the same time. The third statement reports that a certain word is applicable to the shapes of both pennies. Are these three ways of describing the relationship between the shapes of the two pennies really different? In what sense, if any, may only one of them be considered correct? Which one constitutes the correct or true description of the relationship?

Clearly, such questions as these are relevant to the relationship of any quality or characteristic of one individual thing and a quality or characteristic of another individual thing which can be described as resembling, or as identical, or as objects of the applicability of the same general word. I shall refer to this kind of relationship as "the recurrence of a quality"; this locution will be used as a neutral technical term, although ordinarily it would suggest the second kind of description. I shall refer to the qualities so-related as "the instances of the recurrent quality." But the use of this phrase should not be interpreted as a commitment to the view that there is one quality which is instantiated in distinct individual things at the same time. To be committed to this view is already to be committed to the description of the recurrence of a quality as a kind of identity. Nor should it be supposed that by "instances of a recurrent quality" is meant the individual things which are characterized by this quality. Recurrence is a relationship between qualities of individual things, not between individual things themselves. Indeed, in addition to saying that the shape of one penny resembles the shape of another penny, we are entitled to say that the one penny resembles the other penny (in respect to shape). But we are so entitled, presumably, only because we recognize that the *shape* of the one penny resembles or is the same as the *shape* of the other penny.[2] And while it would be proper also to say that the shape of the one penny and the shape of the other are one and the same (i.e., are identical), it would not be proper to say that the one penny and the other penny are one and the same. A technical term such as "recurrence of quality" is needed because there is no equivalent nontechnical expression that is neutral with respect to the three possible descriptions of a relationship such as that between the shapes of two pennies. This is not surprising. Perhaps, if there had been such an expression, there would have been no puzzle about the relationship.

In this essay I shall be concerned with the question of the proper description of the recurrence of qualities. It is a clearer version of the question whether the qualities of individual things are universal or particular. And this latter question seems to contain whatever clear, significant, and distinctive content there may be in the traditional question whether there are universals. According to the Resemblance Theory of universals, the instances of a recurrent quality are distinct particular qualities related by a relation of resemblance. According to the Identity Theory, they constitute an identical quality which is present in distinct individual things at the same time. According to the Nominalist Theory, they

2. See below, p. 37 and pp. 104-105.

are related only by the fact that they are objects of the applicability of one and the same general word. To say that there are universals is, I suggest, to say that the Identity Theory is true.

It should be emphasized that the question of the proper description of the recurrence of qualities is not whether there are qualitatively indistinguishable qualities in distinct things. Even if the red color of one thing is *qualitatively* indistinguishable from the red color of another thing (which they need not be in order to be instances of a recurrent quality—they could be one and the same *general* color, i.e., red), one can still ask whether the two are one and the same quality or two distinct qualities that are exactly alike. That there could be such qualitatively indistinguishable qualities of individual things would seem undeniable, though some philosophers have denied it, probably by confusing this assertion with the assertion that two such qualities are identical. Nor should we take seriously the quick claim that the very statement of the question already entails the answer that such qualities cannot be identical. Indeed, there is something paradoxical about asking whether two qualities, which can be identified separately (by reference to the distinct things to which they belong) and thus can be distinguished, are identical. But this is precisely the paradox which gives rise to the problem of universals. The whole point is that such qualities seem distinguishable and yet, *in so far as they are qualities,* there seems to be no difference between them. That they cannot be identical would require considerable argument. The defenders of the Identity Theory, even if mistaken, have not merely committed an elementary logical blunder. Nevertheless, what has made such a quick rejection of the Identity Theory appear plausible is the vagueness of the question whether the qualities of individual things are universal or particular. Unless it is understood as concerning the proper description of the recurrence of qualities, it is unclear what would be meant by a universal quality or by a particular quality, and it may be tempting to interpret the question as demanding whether a quality of one individual thing and a quality of another individual thing can be *qualitatively* indistinguishable (the obvious answer being that they can), or whether they can be *completely* (and not just qualitatively) indistinguishable (the obvious answer now being that they cannot). However, "universal" and "particular" are technical philosophical terms, and a statement of the problem of universals must not start with them; rather, it must start by explaining the philosophical issue that suggests their introduction, and the precise sense that they are to have. Otherwise, the problem of universals would be unintelligible (if the terms "universal" and "particular" are left unexplained) or philosophically trivial (if it is understood to concern the possibility of either qualitative or complete indistinguishability of qualities of distinct individual things).

It seems clear that despite the great differences among "accidental" qualities such as colors or shapes, "substantive" qualities such as felinity, relations such as larger-than, and numerical qualities such as being a pair, they can all enter in the relation of recurrence in exactly the same sense. The question whether the instances of felinity are identical or merely similar can be dealt with in exactly the same way and in accordance with exactly the same considerations as the question whether the instances of the color red in certain individual things are identical or merely similar. For, according to the terminology proposed here, an instance of felinity is not an individual cat but the latter's characteristic of being a cat, just as an instance of the color red is not a red thing but the latter's red color. This is not to presuppose any particular theory of the principle of individuation (e.g., that it is matter, or spatiotemporal location, or a certain necessarily unique combination of instances of universals) or of the nature of substantive qualities (e.g., that they are, or that they are not, reducible to mere collections of accidental qualities), but it is to acknowledge the necessity of *some* principle of individuation. Whatever the nature of the individuality or thinghood of a certain particular cat, and whatever the proper account of felinity, the cat itself cannot *constitute* an instance of felinity. For, in addition to being a cat, it must be distinguishable from any other cat. And that in virtue of which it is so distinguishable cannot then be part of what it is to be a cat. This may become clearer if we note the applicability of the argument even to a world consisting, not of things or substances, but of sense-data, say, color-patches. A blue color-patch contains or is characterized by an instance of the color blue (as well as of a number of other recurrent qualities, e.g., circularity). But the patch itself cannot *constitute* such an instance. For it must be distinguishable from other blue color-patches. And that in virtue of which it is so distinguishable (presumably its spatiotemporal location, and perhaps also shape) cannot be part of what it is to be blue.

Again, the relationship that holds between the relation of a certain book and a certain fountain pen which can be described as the former's being larger than the latter, and the relation of a certain table and a certain typewriter which also can be described as the former's being larger than the latter, is, from the point of view of the problem of universals, quite the same as the peculiar relationship that holds between the color of a book and the color of a fountain pen which can be described as their identity, or resemblance, or as their being objects of the applicability of the same general word; thus the second-order relationship can be described as the identity of the first-order relations, or as their resemblance, or as their being objects of the applicability of the same general relational term. Nor is the case of the recurrence of "numerical qualities" different. Indeed, if there is an irreducible category of numerical quality at all, it would be fundamentally different from the other categories of quality in that a numerical quality is necessarily a quality of a *collection* of things. The quality of being a pair characterizes the collection of hats on the rack, not a certain hat. But, however important this difference may be for other philosophical inquiries, it does not affect in any way the description of the recurrence of such qualities. It is obvious that there is a certain relationship between the collection of hats on the rack and the collection of pencils on my desk which can be described by saying that they, as collections, have an identical quality, or (exactly) similar qualities, or are objects of the applicability of the general term "pair," and that the choice of the proper description of this relationship would be determined in the same way as it would be with respect to the recurrence of colors or shapes. What is not obvious, of course, is that it is the existence of such qualities that mathematics seems to require, and indeed that mathematics requires the existence of anything at all. But these questions belong to the philosophy of mathematics, and not to the theory of universals. If the entities whose existence mathematics may require are not qualities at all (and if they are, they would, presumably, be qualities of *collections*), then they may still present a challenge to the empiricist; but the mere fact that they would be regarded as unobservable, nonspatiotemporal, and in general rather mysterious would hardly be a reason for classifying them as universals.

The very existence of Nominalism as a serious theory of the recurrence of qualities suggests that there is an intimate connection between the concept of recurrence of qualities and the use of general words, such as "circular," "hat," "larger-than," "pair." As we shall see in Chapter One, even if the Nominalist Theory is false, it would still seem true that one can think of all the instances of a recurrent quality only if one thinks of the range of applicability of a certain general word: one can think of the color qualities of all blue things only if one thinks of the range of applicability of the word "blue." And if this is so, it may seem natural to conclude that what alone suggests to us the fact of the recurrences of qualities and makes it seem philosophically important is that certain words, which are essential to the expression of our knowledge of the world, are applicable to a number of individual things. Consequently, the theorist of universals may consider that his primary task is to present an account of the applicability of general words. And the use of such words is puzzling. A general word is applicable neither to only one object, nor to a definite, enumerable group of objects, but to an indefinite number of objects. Yet, ordinarily, its meaning is quite determinate and there is a clear distinction between the objects to which it is applicable and the objects to which it is not. What, then, determines the range of the objects to which it is applicable? How do we recognize an object as one to which a certain general word is applicable? What makes classification of objects possible? This is the problem of the explanation of the applicability of general words, which is another version of the philosophical problem of universals, and the Resemblance Theory, the Identity Theory, and the Nominalist Theory can also be regarded as proposed solutions of this problem, the first theory providing an explanation of the applicability of a general word by asserting that the objects to which the word applies resemble each other, the second providing such an explanation by asserting that these objects have a common quality, and the third simply repeating that the word is applicable to the objects.

Now it may seem that there is no genuine distinction between the problem of the recurrence of qualities and that of the applicability of general words. Indeed, this is the explicit claim of both the Identity and the Resemblance Theory as theories of the applicability of general words. The problem is to explain why certain words are applicable to an indefinite number of objects within a certain determinate range. But, one would think, the only reason any word, once it has a determinate meaning, is applicable to a certain object or to a number of objects is the nature, or characteristics, or properties of the object or objects. Indeed, one can be puzzled about the nature of the meaning of a word, the way in which its meaning is determined, the kind of relation it has to the objects to which it is applicable. But these are questions which concern any word, and not only general words. They ought not to be confused with the problem of universals, which is concerned with general words because of a feature peculiar to them, namely, their re-applicability, the peculiar extension of their applicability to objects with respect to which the word has not been, and perhaps could not have been, learned.[3] The problem of the explanation of the applicability of general words would thus be reduced to the problem of the relationship of the natures, characteristics, or properties of the objects to which the same general word is applicable. And this is the problem of the recurrence of qualities, which the Identity Theory would solve by describing the relationship as one of identity and which the Resemblance Theory would solve by describing it as resemblance. Their concern with the applicability of general words or with the possibility of classification in general would thus be merely an extension, an incidental consequence, of their concern with the description of the recurrence of qualities, which would be the fundamental task of the theorist of universals. But such a conclusion is not at all obviously correct. It requires detailed argument, to which I shall devote the entire first chapter. For the main claim of one of the three theories of universals is precisely that such a conclusion is false. As an explanation of the applicability of general words, the Nominalist Theory would claim that no ref-

3. See below, section 2.

erence to the recurrence of a quality resolves the puzzling nature of the applicability of general words. And as a theory of the description of recurrences, it would attempt to reduce the fact of the recurrence of a quality to the fact that a certain general word is in use. Only if the Nominalist Theory is false in both of its versions may we assume that the question concerning the applicability of general words is reducible to that of the correct description of the recurrence of qualities. In Chapter One we shall begin with the first version, but we shall discover that the strongest arguments for Nominalism are to be found in its second version. And the main argument of this essay will be resumed in Chapter Two.

The Nominalist Theory
/one

2. *The Explanation of the Applicability of General Words*

What seems to require explanation in the applicability of a general word, such as "blue," is not so much the fact that such a word applies, or can be used to apply, to each of a collection of individual objects, e.g., to blue things, but that its applicability or meaning is not limited to any *particular* collecton of individual objects, e.g., to a book, fountain pen, and coat, by reference to which one may have learned the meaning of the word "blue" originally. A necessary condition of one's knowing the meaning of a general word is one's ability to apply it correctly to objects which one has never encountered before. But, then, to know the meaning of a general word such as "blue" is not merely to know that it applies to a certain finite number of objects such as the exemplars of the meaning of the word (in someone's case: a certain book, a certain fountain pen, and a certain coat). Perhaps one cannot know its meaning without also knowing that the word applies to certain

16

objects which one can readily identify and enumerate. But neither is knowing that the word applies to certain such objects the same as knowing the meaning of the word. One knows the meaning of a general word only if one can *recognize* a newly encountered object, e.g., a blue hat, as one to which the word applies. Now the problem of the explanation of the applicability of general words is the question, "What is that in a newly encountered object, in virtue of which one recognizes that object as one to which a certain general word applies?" The Identity Theory would answer this question by asserting that the newly encountered object (e.g., the blue hat) and the exemplars of the meaning of the word (e.g., a book, a fountain pen, and a coat) have a common quality (e.g., the color blue). The Resemblance Theory would answer it by asserting that the newly encountered object resembles the exemplars of the meaning of the general word at least as closely as the exemplars resemble one another.[1] But a third theory of the applicability of general words, the Nominalist Theory, would answer the question platitudinously by asserting that the newly encountered object is recognized as one to which the word applies only because the word does apply to it. The blue hat is recognized as one to which the word "blue" applies only because the word "blue" does apply to it, i.e., only because it is blue. Indeed, the Nominalist Theory would not identify the *applicability* of a word to certain objects with the actual fact of its *being applied* to these objects. Such an identification would not merely make the theory quite implausible—it would

1. Cf. H. H. Price, *Thinking and Experience*, Chapter 1. For full references to works cited see Bibliography.

make it unintelligible. The notion of general word is inseparable from the notion of its applicability to objects to which it has never been actually applied and perhaps will never be applied. And it is this feature of general words that gives rise to philosophical puzzlement. The Nominalist Theory may hold that there is no cause for such puzzlement, but it cannot hold, in effect, that there are no general words. However, the fact that a defensible version of the Nominalist Theory must recognize the notion of the *applicability* of general words does not mean that it tacitly endorses the Identity or the Resemblance Theory. For the interesting claim of the theory is that no genuine explanation of the applicability of general words can be given, that although a general word is applicable even to objects to which it has never been in fact applied, there is still nothing more that can be said about such objects than simply that the word is applicable to them.

The Nominalist Theory begins by pointing out that ordinarily the applicability of a general word to certain objects is explained in terms of the applicability to these objects of other general words. For instance, one might explain the applicability of the word "man" to *a, b,* and *c* by saying that *a, b,* and *c* are animals and that they are rational. No such explanation is relevant to the philosophical problem of the applicability of general words, because it is either incomplete, in that it uses general words, the applicability of which demands just as much explanaton, or circular, in that eventually it uses the general words the applicability of which is to be explained. An adequate explanation must, so to speak, break through the limits of language. Yet, clearly,

it cannot be ostensive. The listing or showing of paradigms of the application of a general word *may* succeed
in teaching a person to what objects the word is applicable, but it cannot constitute a logically complete explanation of the applicability of the word. For, knowing
that the word is applicable to the objects given as paradigms is not a *sufficient* condition of knowing to what
other objects it is applicable. On the other hand, any
attempt to explain the applicability of a general word
by reference to a certain fact about all of the objects to
which it is applicable would either not succeed in explaining anything at all because it would fail to identify
the fact to which the explanation appeals; or else it
would provide a circular and thus uninformative explanation by identifying the fact which is supposed to
explain the applicability of the word by using the very
word whose applicability is to be explained.[2] Consider

2. Cf. D. F. Pears, "Universals," *Philosophical Quarterly*, 1950-51;
Stuart Hampshire, *Thought and Action*, and "Scepticism and Meaning," *Philosophy*, 1950; J. O. Urmson, "Recognition," *Proceedings of
the Aristotelian Society*, 1955-56. Anthony Quinton, in "Properties and
Classes," *Proceedings of the Aristotelian Society*, 1957-58, presents a
much milder version of the theory; he argues for the distinction between natural and arbitrary classes by appealing to the fact *about language* that not all words are reapplicable. Quinton's statement of the
problem of the explanation of the applicability of general words is
probably the clearest one in the literature on the subject. A similar but
more far-reaching view is defended by J. R. Bambrough in "Universals
and Family Resemblances," *Proceedings of the Aristotelian Society*,
1960-61. He argues that "Wittgenstein solved [in his remarks about
"family resemblances"] what is known as 'the problem of universals,'"
by agreeing both with the nominalist tenet that "there is no limit to
the number of possible classifications of objects" and also with the
realist tenet that "there is no classification of any set of objects which
is not objectively based on genuine similarities and differences." I
shall examine the Nominalist part of this view in section 4. The notion
of "family resemblances" itself, as distinct from what I must regard as

the word "blue." Both the Identity Theory and the Resemblance Theory hold that there is a fact about all objects that are called blue which is distinct from the fact that they are called blue and which yet constitutes the explanation of the latter fact: the fact in question may be the presence in all blue things of a certain common quality or the resemblance of certain qualities of all blue things. But *which* common quality? *What* resemblance? Clearly, the Identity Theory and the Resemblance Theory must identify, respectively, the common quality and the resemblance to which they appeal in their explanation of the applicability of the word "blue," for, only a certain kind of common quality or resemblance would explain the applicability of the word "blue." And how can the Identity Theory identify the relevant quality of blue things except by using the word "blue"? How can the Resemblance Theory identify the relevant resemblance of certain qualities of blue things except by using the word "blue"? The two traditional theories of the applicability of general words are essentially circular. They only seem to explain the applicability of the word "blue." And it might actually be more helpful if one were to say simply that certain things are called blue because they are blue.

Now it seems clear that were this the really serious Nominalist argument, the Nominalist Theory should be rejected forthwith. For the argument rests on an obvious confusion between the question, "How can one

----

Bambrough's extension of it, suggests no particular theory about the reapplicability of a general word (e.g., "game"), and, with respect to what I have called the recurrence of qualities, seems to belong with the Resemblance Theory.

explain the meaning of a general word, e.g., the word
'blue'?" and the question, "Why is a general word applied to objects other than those by reference to which
its meaning was originally determined?" Indeed, there
is a sense in which a noncircular and logically complete
answer to the *first* question is impossible and thus a
claim of the Identity or the Resemblance Theory to
provide one would be false. *In a sense,* the explanation
of the meaning of a general word would be logically
incomplete if it were stated entirely in words other than
the word to be explained; for these other words would
need explanation too. And it would be circular, if it
achieved completeness by explaining the meaning of
the word through the use of the word to be explained.
An ostensive explanation would also be incomplete because it would necessarily fail to explain the applicability
of the word to objects other than those referred to in the
explanation. But there is nothing obviously illegitimate
in a philosophical attempt to answer the *second* question. Suppose we ask, why is the word "blue," the meaning of which, let us assume, has been learned by reference to this book and that coat, applicable also to this
hat and that wall? To answer by saying, "Because the
hat and the wall are blue," is, of course, to offer a
platitudinous answer, for the very statement of the
question already presupposes that the hat and the wall
are blue. But such a platitudinous answer is neither the
only possible one nor the one which philosophers have
been interested in. One could also say, "Because their
color is the same as that of the book and the coat" or
"Because their colors resemble those of the book and
the coat sufficiently." It may be true that one cannot

identify the "same color" or the "resemblance" in question without using the word "blue." But, first, why should one identify them at all? One is not trying to *teach* anyone the meaning of the word "blue." And, second, why should one not identify them by using the word "blue"? One is not attempting a definition of the word "blue."

The reason for the confusion of the above two questions is perhaps the ambiguity of the phrases "explanation of the meaning of general words" and "explanation of naming." Sometimes it is convenient to use such phrases in a brief statement of the problem of the explanation of the applicability of general words. But to suppose that the question, "Do universals exist?" amounts, in this case, to the question, "What is the appropriate comprehensive explanation of naming?" is to involve the problem of universals in the difficulties of the general problem of meaning and of the nature of the relationship of language to the world. Such an involvement is justified neither by sound argument nor by the history of the problem of universals. There is no reason why the theorist of universals should be concerned with issues such as "How and why do words apply to objects?" or "What is the best analogue of the relationship between a word and the objects to which it applies?" His proper concern, in so far as he is interested in the meaning of general words at all, is surely only the question, "In virtue of what fact about a certain object is a certain general word applicable to it?" And this is really the question, "In virtue of what fact about a certain group of objects is it possible to apply to all of them one and the same word, whatever this word may actually be?" What puzzles the theorist of universals is not at all the nature of the relationship of a certain word to the objects of its application, but the extendability of this relationship, the fact that if the word has this relationship to objects *a*, *b*, and *c*, it just as clearly has the same relationship also to objects *d, e, f*. And there seems to be nothing obviously illegitimate or circular in accounting for this fact by saying that *d, e, f* . . . resemble or have an identical quality with *a, b,* and *c*.

In general, theories of universals are not attempts to explain the meaning of general words. But they may be attempts to explain the *possibility* of the meaning of general words.[3] The fact that there is a sense in which one cannot give a logically complete, noncircular, and yet nonostensive answer to the question, "What does a certain general word mean?" does not imply that one cannot give a logically complete, noncircular, and non-ostensive answer to the question, "What is the fact about certain objects that makes it possible and important for us to refer to them with one and the same word?" For, that in the world which makes the use of a certain general word possible may be a *necessary* condition of the use or meaning of the word, but it need not be, and in fact it appears obvious that it is not, a *sufficient* condition. It may be that any description of naming involves us in an impossible attempt to transcend language by using language. It may be that we cannot even describe naming by the use of analogy, for perhaps nothing is sufficiently like naming to serve as a useful analogue to

3. Pears notes this distinction but, inexplicably, fails to see its importance and virtually ignores it.

it. But it would not follow that that in the world which makes naming possible cannot be described, or that nothing is sufficiently like *it* in order that it may serve as an analogue to it. The obvious analogue to qualitative identity is the identity of an individual thing through time. As Johnson remains the same man throughout his life, so is the color red the same in all red things. And an analogue to qualitative resemblance might be the relationship of being a member of the same family. As John, Peter, Mary, Susan, and Bill are related by being members of the same family, so are the colors of red things related by their resemblance. But these are matters which must be left for Chapters Two and Three.

The Nominalist Theory, however, is not only a theory of the applicability of general words, but also a theory of the recurrence of qualities. In its former capacity it may be inadequate. But this does not entail that it is also inadequate in its latter capacity. We shall find that its genuine strength lies in its arguments concerning the description of the recurrence of qualities. And what it has not achieved as a theory of the applicability of general words, it may achieve as a theory of the recurrence of qualities. Its goal will be to show that the distinction between naming and that in the world which makes naming possible is illegitimate because the only fact that we can know about that in the world which makes naming possible is that it is that which makes naming possible. And its conclusion will be that the recurrence of a quality is nothing but the fact that a certain general word is in use.

Considered superficially, this conclusion of the Nominalist Theory appears obviously false. In describing certain qualities of individual things as identical or only similar we seem to be describing an independent fact about the world which in no sense is a fact about language. And that there is such a fact about the world, such a relationship among the qualities of individual things, would seem unquestionable. Suppose that I am examining the colors of the blue book, the blue fountain pen, and the blue coat. And then a blue and a red hat are placed before me. I may immediately become aware of a certain relationship between the color of the blue hat and the colors of the book, fountain pen, and coat and of a strikingly different relationship between the color of the red hat and the colors of the book, fountain pen, and coat, without either considering the meaning of the word "blue" or using the word "blue" or knowing how to use the word "blue" or even knowing any language. Of course, one cannot describe such a relationship unless one uses language, but this logical fact would support the Nominalist Theory no more than it would support the claim that every fact we describe must be a fact about language because we cannot describe it without using language. However, the Nominalist Theory of the recurrence of qualities cannot be rejected quite so easily.

As a theory of the applicability of general words, the Nominalist Theory argued (1) that the recurrence of a quality can be identified only by reference to the applicability of a certain general word to its instances, and, therefore, (2) that the recurrence of the quality cannot explain the applicability of that general word to its instances. As a theory concerning the description of the recurrence of qualities, the Nominalist Theory will now present the thesis that either there is no such fact as the recurrence of a quality or the recurrence of a quality is merely the fact that a certain general word is applicable to the instances of the recurrent quality. And it will support this thesis with two distinct arguments. The first can be summarized as follows: (1) we can identify all of the logically possible[4] *instances* of a recurrent quality only by reference to the applicability of a certain general word to all of them; therefore, (2) the only fact that we can know about all of the logically possible instances of a recurrent quality is that a certain general word is applicable to all of them;[5] therefore, (3) either there is no such fact about all of the logically possible instances of the quality as their recurrence, or their recurrence is merely the fact that a certain general word is applicable to all of them. The second argument can be summarized as follows: (1) we can identify the *recurrence* of a recurrent quality only by reference to the applicability of a certain general word to all of the logically possible instances of the recurrent quality; therefore, (2) the only fact that we can know about the recurrence of a quality is that a certain general word is applicable to all of its logically possible instances; therefore, (3) either there is no such fact as the recurrence of a quality or the recurrence of a quality is merely the fact that a certain general word is applicable to all of its logically possible instances. The two arguments differ

4. The reason for speaking of logically possible instances will be explained below, p. 29.

5. And, of course, anything that would be entailed by this (e.g., that the instances of the color blue are instances of color). I shall not mention this irrelevant qualification again, in order to avoid unnecessary complications of verbal expression.

because their premises, which I shall examine in detail shortly, are different. Apart from the truth of its premise, each argument depends on the validity of the inference of step (2) from step (1). The defense of this inference would be the same in both arguments. It can be summarized as follows: If the only way in which we can identify *a* is by reference to the fact that it is *F*, then the only logically distinct fact that we can know or describe about *a* is that it is *F*. For if there were some other fact about *a* that we could know or describe, then *a* would also be identifiable by reference to this other fact. Of course, there is a sense in which it can be said that there may still be such a fact as the recurrence of a quality, even if we cannot know it or describe it. But it is clear that a theory of universals may not be concerned with the description of facts which cannot be known and cannot be described.

3. The First Argument of the Nominalist Theory

The first argument of the Nominalist Theory can be explained as follows. To describe the recurrence of a certain quality, one must be able to identify the instances of the quality. Otherwise, it would be impossible to distinguish the recurrence of this quality from the recurrences of other qualities, or, for that matter, from any other facts in the world. We must know the terms of a relation before we can begin to describe their relation. Now one way in which the instances of a recurrent quality (i.e., the resembling or identical qualities of certain individual things) can be identified is through the use of a general word which applies to them. The colors of blue things, the relation of which we may wish to describe, can be identified simply as blue. There is nothing objectionable about this kind of identification as such, for it is not with the name of the quality that we are concerned but with its recurrence. But if the instances of a recurrent quality can be identified *only* through the use of an appropriate general word, then such an identification would be objectionable. For then there would be no distinct fact about all of the instances of a certain quality which can be described as their resemblance or identity, since if there had been such a fact it would have been possible that the instances of the quality be identified by reference to it and not by reference to the word which applies to them. Now the number of logically possible instances of a recurrent quality and of kinds of individual things which they may qualify is unlimited. There can be no logical limitation on the number and kinds of things which can instantiate a quality, as long as such instantiation is not logically incompatible with the presence in the same individual thing of another quality. Indeed, a quality for which it is logically impossible to have one more instance than it already has would not be a quality at all. But how can one identify all logically possible instances of a recurrent quality? Clearly, only by reference to the applicability of the same general word to all of them. There is nothing else that one can possibly know about an unlimited number of actual and merely logically possible qualities of individual things. Consequently, the relationship of the instances of the quality which we have called its recurrence can only be, if it is at all describable, the applicability to all of them of the same general word.

But may not one be concerned only with some actual instances of a recurrent quality which can be identified independently of the applicability to them of a certain general word? And may not one attempt then to describe the recurrence of the quality? Suppose that there are only two individual things which are blue. If these individual things are independently identifiable, their colors can be identified by reference to them and then any relationship of the two colors, such as their recurrence, can be described independently of the fact that they are called blue. But the description of such a relation would not be the description of the recurrence of the *color blue*. For it would still be logically possible that there is a third individual that is blue. And would then the description of the recurrence of the color blue in the first two individuals be necessarily true of the recurrence of the color blue in all three individuals? If it would not, then we cannot say that the description of the relationship of the colors of the first two individuals has been the description of the recurrence of the color blue. If it would, then what we have described may only be the fact that all three colors are correctly called blue. For the only fact about the color of the third individual that we have assumed is that it is correctly called blue; and if this fact is sufficient to indicate that the relationship of this color to the colors of the first two individuals must be the same as the relationship of the colors of the first two individuals alone, then such a relationship is a mere feature or consequence of the fact that all three are correctly called blue. To describe this relationship as the sameness or resemblance of certain qualities would be merely another way of saying that one and the same general word is applicable to all of them. If one can identify the colors of the blue and red hat and the colors of the book, fountain pen, and coat only as blue or as red, clearly the only fact about these colors that there is to be described is that the color of the one hat is blue, the color of the other red, and the colors of the book, fountain pen, and coat, blue. There is no other fact to be described because there is no fact about the so-identified relata other than that some of them are correctly called blue and one is correctly called red. Consequently, there is no such fact as the recurrence of the color blue, unless it is simply that certain things are correctly called blue. There is no problem of the description of the recurrence of qualities because there is nothing to be so described, or if there is, it cannot be described. There is only the fact that a certain general word has a use.

The above argument of the Nominalist Theory against the possibility of an independent description of the recurrence of qualities is important, but invalid. What has made it convincing is that we have thought of the description of the recurrence of the color blue as the description of the relationship of the colors of *all* (actual and logically possible) blue things. But the only fact about the colors of all blue things is the fact that they all would be correctly called blue. Therefore, there can be no independent description of the relationship of the colors of *all* blue things. This is the important, and perhaps true, claim of the Nominalist Theory. And, naturally, we have thought that if this claim is true, then there can be no independent description of the recurrence of the color blue. For we have assumed all along that to describe the recurrence of a quality is to describe the relationship of *all* of the instances of this quality. But it is not necessary to make such an assumption. It seems necessary only because we still fail to see that the problem of the description of the recurrence of qualities is very different from the problem of the explanation of the meaning of general words. One cannot explain the meaning of a general word unless one explains its meaning in respect to all objects to which it can be properly applied. But in order to answer the question whether the colors of blue things are one and the same color or distinct particular colors which resemble each other, we need not be concerned with the relationship of the colors of all blue things. What is interesting about this question has nothing to do with the *number* of blue things with the relationship of whose colors we are concerned. For the question is not whether in fact certain objects, e.g., all blue things, have a common quality or have particular qualities which resemble each other, but whether it is *possible* for more than one thing to have one and the same quality. So the relationship of the colors of two blue things is just as interesting from this point of view as the relationship of the colors of all actual and merely logically possible blue things. And while the description of the latter relationship is involved in the difficulty of our inability to identify the colors of *all* (actual and possible) blue things in any other way except as blue, the description of the former relationship is completely free from this difficulty. The reason for this is that the colors of two (or three or four) blue things *can* be identified ostensively, or by reference to the independently identifiable individuals which they characterize, and not solely by reference to the fact that they are called blue. One can describe the relationship of the color of the blue hat and the colors of the book, fountain pen, and coat without even knowing the meaning of the word "blue" because one can identify the colors of the hat, the book, the fountain pen, and the coat by pointing to them or by their different positions in one's visual field, or by the shapes with which they are associated, or by reference to the hat, book, fountain pen, and coat themselves. Even if one did not possess the concepts of hat, book, fountain pen, and coat, in addition to not possessing the concepts of blue and red, one could still, and equally intelligently, notice and attempt to describe the peculiar fact about the colors of the two hats and the colors of the book, fountain pen, and coat, namely, that the color of one of the hats is the same as, or resembles, the colors of the book, fountain pen, and coat, while the color of the other hat is not the same as, or does not resemble, the colors of the book, fountain pen, and coat. And then one could properly ask whether one and the same color is present in the different objects or whether different colors are present which resemble each other. It should be noted that in arguing for the possibility of identifying qualities of individuals independently of the fact that certain general words apply to them, I am not arguing that qualities of individuals are not dependent for their identification upon the identification of some other objects, e.g., individuals. I am arguing for only one kind of independence of their identification, namely, independence of the fact that certain general words apply to them.

4. *The Second Argument of the Nominalist Theory*

According to the second argument of the Nominalist Theory, there is no such relation as the resemblance or recurrence of qualities which is distinct from the fact that a certain general word is applicable to the qualities, even if the *terms* of such a relation could be identified independently of the fact that a certain general word is applicable to them. The distinctive claim of the second argument is that the *recurrence* of the recurrent quality is itself identifiable only by reference to the applicability of a certain general word to its terms, and, therefore, that the only possible fact that we can know about the recurrence of a quality is that a certain general word is applicable to its instances. Consequently, we cannot reject the second argument of the Nominalist Theory in the way in which we have rejected its first argument. For the second argument does not depend on a claim concerning the method of identification of the *instances* of a recurrent quality, but on a claim concerning the method of identification of the *recurrence* of these instances.

The main thesis of the argument is that every object resembles every other object in some respect; that there is no clear reason for supposing that resemblances in some respects are naturally greater or more important than resemblances in other respects; that the only possible way in which one can single out a resemblance of two objects is by noticing that this resemblance has already been singled out in language, i.e., that the resembling objects are already describable with the same word, or at least that the existing classificatory system of language determines our decision to institute a new term, and thus establish a new class, by determining the general conditions of classification in our particular language, the sorts of resemblances that "should be" noticed. If every object resembles every other object, then to assert that certain objects resemble each other is to make an empty statement unless the assertion is complemented (explicitly or implicitly, through the context) with an indication of the respect in which these objects resemble each other, i.e., unless a general word applicable to them is indicated. Considered alone, the statement "The book resembles the fountain pen" says nothing, except perhaps that the book and the fountain pen exist. Such statements become complete only if the respect of the resemblance is stated. But to state the respect of the resemblance of two objects is to classify the two objects, to apply a certain general word to both of them. This can be done in two ways. The respect can be stated specifically, as in "The book resembles the fountain pen in being pink," and then it is clear that the resemblance is nothing but the fact that both of its terms are correctly describable with the general word "pink." Or the respect can be stated generically, as in "The book resembles the fountain pen in color," and while such an assertion does not consist in the assertion that a certain general word is applicable to both terms, it does consist in the assertion that one of a certain range of general words is applicable to both terms.

If the book resembles the fountain pen in color, this does not tell us that both are pink. But it does tell us that *some* specific color-word is applicable to both. But, one may ask, can we not notice the resemblance in question without noticing that certain general words are applicable to both of its terms? Yet, what would noticing a resemblance be? What possible information could be conveyed by the statement that the book and the fountain pen resemble each other? What explanation of such a statement can one give other than that certain general words are applicable to both the book and the fountain pen?

I think that there are two distinct claims behind the general assertion that merely to say that two objects resemble each other is to make a vacuous statement, that a relation of resemblance can be identified only by reference to the applicability of the same general word to its terms. The first is that any terms of a relation of resemblance are infinitely complex, in the sense that there can be no logical limit to the number of characteristics they have and to the relations they enter. The second claim, however, is that even if there is no such complexity in the terms of the resemblance, the mere assertion that they resemble each other is still uninformative. For one can always ask, what is meant by such an assertion, and the person making the assertion can explain its meaning only by mentioning the general word or words applicable to both terms. An assertion about a relation of resemblance is informative only in so far as it can lead to, or be interpreted as, an assertion that certain general words apply to both terms of the resemblance. But this implies that there is no relation of resemblance, no fact of the recurrence of qualities, which is distinct from, and independent of, the fact that there are general words in use. Let us begin with the first claim.

According to it, a statement of the form "*x* resembles *y*" is incomplete; by itself such a statement is quite uninformative, because every object resembles every other object in some respect. And, indeed, as long as by object here one means an individual, such as a man, a table, or a city, this claim must be accepted. It is only a way of reasserting the traditional view that the nature of the individual is inexhaustible. An individual is a three-dimensional persistent object. It necessarily enters in spatial relations with every other individual. It has a history and preserves its identity through qualitative and quantitative change. The number of its characteristics is unlimited. To assert barely that an individual resembles another individual is to assert that the resemblance is in respect to one of this unlimited number of characteristics. It follows that it is essential to the meaningfulness of a statement about the resemblance of certain objects that their resemblance be identified in some way as *this* resemblance and not another of the unlimited number of ways in which the objects may resemble. But how can a resemblance of certain objects be identified except by stating its respect? And what can stating the respect in which certain objects resemble be, other than stating that a certain general word (or one of a certain range of general words) applies to these objects? The only possible way to identify the resemblance of two objects is by the use of a general word, either specific or generic. And if this is so, then the resemblance collapses into the mere fact that a certain word is used to apply to both objects. For, as we have seen, if the only way in which one can identify something is by reference to its being F or having F or being related to F, then the only logically distinct fact about it that one can know is that it is F or has F or is related to F.

But it is not only individuals which can be said to resemble each other. So can the qualities or characteristics of individuals. The very argument intended to show that all resemblance of individuals must be resemblance in a certain respect also shows that all resemblance of individuals must be the resemblance of certain qualities of the individuals. For to specify the respect in which two individuals resemble each other is to specify the quality of the one and the quality of the other which themselves must be said to resemble each other. If two books are said to resemble each other in respect to color, this is to say that the color of the one resembles the color of the other. If two men are said to resemble each other in respect to intelligence, this is to say that the intelligence of the one resembles the intelligence of the other. But then the question arises whether it is also true of the resemblance of qualities that it must be in some respect, i.e., that it must be identified by means of a general word. And it seems that it is not. For a quality does not have the inexhaustible nature of an individual. Consider colors, shapes, sounds, even smells and tastes. Perhaps not all such sensuous qualities are as simple as they often have been supposed to be. There is good reason to regard color as constituted by the three factors of hue, saturation, and brilliance; shape as constituted by size and geometrical figure; sound as constituted by pitch, loudness, and timbre; smell and taste perhaps as constituted by a specific nature (e.g., sourness), intensity, and purity. But even if some specific sensuous qualities are complex, their complexity is quite distinct from that of individuals. The number of characteristics of, or factors in, a specific sensuous quality is quite limited; and these characteristics or factors of qualities seem to hide no further complexity. But with the diminishing degree of complexity in objects which are said to resemble each other, the need of specifying the respect of the resemblance diminishes. Perhaps to assert that the color of *a* is like the color of *b* would still be misleading, because the two colors may resemble each other in respect to hue but not in respect to brilliance. But will any ambiguity be found in asserting that the hue of the color of *a* is like the hue of the color of *b*, or is more like the hue of the color of *b* than it is like the hue of the color of *c*? Or that the pitch of a certain sound is like the pitch of some other sound (though the loudnesses and timbres of the two sounds differ)? Indeed, it would seem idle to ask in what respect are the hue of this color and the hue of that color alike, or in what respect are the pitch of this sound and the pitch of that sound alike.

Clearly, therefore, there are cases of resemblance in which no specification of a respect is needed. And what is even more important is that these cases of resemblance are not isolated or exceptional, but constitute the basis of all other cases of resemblance. For the resemblances that need no specification of respect are the resemblances of simple qualities or of the simple characteristics or factors of complex qualities; and it seems that it is a logical truth that any other kind of resemblance, namely resemblances between individuals and resemblances between complex characteristics, must be reducible to resemblances of the first kind, namely, to resemblances between simple characteristics.

But are we not assuming that there are absolute simples? Are we not presupposing that there is an absolute criterion of simplicity? The word "simple" has many uses, and for some such uses an object would be complex while for others it would be simple. What would be called simple for some purposes would not be called simple for other purposes. Whether an object is simple depends on the particular sense of "simple" which we adopt in describing such an object. But this argument should hardly be considered conclusive. All that it proves is that the word "simple" has no absolutely precise and eternally determined meaning. But this is true of all words, although the exceptional generality of the words "simple" and "composite" makes it especially obvious with regard to them. It is true of "man" and of "red' and of "book." Yet it would hardly be profitable, on account of this fact about language, to argue that nothing can be said, absolutely and unconditionally, to be a man, red in color, or a book. What the argument confuses is two entirely distinct questions, (1) whether the word "simple" has a natural, unchanging, perfectly precise meaning, and (2) whether, for any one criterion of the use of the word "simple," there are objects which can be said, in accordance with that criterion, to be absolutely and unconditionally simple. The first question must be answered negatively. But the second question must be answered affirmatively. The

sense of "simple" in which one would ordinarily call
white simple is quite different from the sense in which
someone with technical knowledge would call white a
composite of the colors of the rainbow. And in the
former sense white *is* simple, while in the latter it *is not*.
But there is nothing particularly important about this
fact, as distinct from the corresponding facts about all
other words in language. The philosophical puzzles
about the existence of absolute simples do not depend
on ignorance of this fact. They depend on the difficulty
of determining whether, in a certain already chosen
sense of "simple," certain objects are simple or any objects are simple.

Nevertheless, in asserting that two qualities resemble
each other and denying that it is necessary to specify the
respect of their resemblance, we are presupposing that
such qualities are simple in one of the senses of "simple."
Does it follow, then, that in presupposing such a sense
of "simple" we are doing in a disguised manner precisely what we claim not to be doing, namely, specifying
the respect of the resemblance? Does not the classification of a quality as simple amount to choosing to consider only one of its characteristics and thus ignoring
its complexity? Through the choice of a particular criterion of simplicity, have we not made the resemblance
even of qualities dependent upon our linguistic system
and thus incapable of independent description? I do not
think so. The strength of the argument against the independent description of recurrences depended on the
claim that to assert that two entities resemble each other
requires at least the implicit specification of the respect
of their resemblance, i.e., requires that a general word

applicable to both be indicated. Now, however, this has become the much weaker claim that any assertion of the resemblance of two entities which does not require a specification of the respect of the resemblance presupposes the adoption of a particular criterion of simplicity —for only if we assume that two qualities are simple would the assertion of their resemblance be free from the requirement that the respect of the resemblance be specified. And I think that there is nothing wrong with making such a presupposition, as long as we do not arbitrarily change the sense of "simple" in different cases of its application. First, even if the correctness of our classification of *a* and *b* as simple is a necessary condition of the truth of our assertion that *a* resembles *b* and that no specification of the respect of their resemblance is necessary, it is not a sufficient condition: *a* and *b* may be simple and yet not resemble each other. And to the extent to which it is not a sufficient condition, the resemblance of *a* and *b* is an independent matter of fact, quite distinct from any fact about language, such as the sense in which we are using the word "simple" or the fact that both *a* and *b* are called blue. Second, the particular way in which we regard two resembling objects when we classify them as "simple" is not necessarily due to our adoption of a particular sense of "simple" in making such a classification. Such a way of regarding an object may be quite independent of the use of the word "simple." In fact, the particular sense of the word "simple" merely reflects the possibility of such a way of regarding an object. Consider the color white. In one sense of the word "simple" it would be simple. What is this sense? It is what may be called the phenomenological sense, the criterion of which is direct observation. To say that white is simple in this sense is to say that one does not directly observe any distinguishable parts in the color white. But white can be said to be a composite if one takes "simple" in a sense, the criterion of which is the manner in which the quality that is to be classified as simple or composite was obtained, in this case the manner being, perhaps, a certain physical experiment. These two senses of "simple" determine two ways in which one can regard white. But this does not mean that one cannot regard white in these two ways without the existence of the word "simple" or its synonymous expressions. One can be interested in the direct appearance of the color white or in the way in which it was obtained even without the use of language. The distinctions of language merely reflect such differences in the ways in which we may regard objects; they do not create them.

The above discussion does not imply that if *a* and *b* are simple qualities we cannot say, for instance, that in addition to their direct resemblance *a* and *b* resemble also in that both are colors liked by Mary, or that they resemble also in that both would be suitable for a certain color effect in the decoration of a room. It seems clear, however, that these two kinds of resemblance are quite different. G. E. Moore calls the one, external resemblance, and the other, internal. He suggests what the difference between them is by saying, "the two (i.e., resembling things) may resemble one another in respect of the fact that they have some common property—some common relation to other things, yet, *in themselves* or internally, they are quite unlike." [6] As long as Moore speaks of external resemblances as being in respect to some common property, the distinction remains unclear. But once it is specified that such a common property is a common relation to other things, the vagueness in the distinction disappears. External resemblance is resemblance in respect to a relation to an entity or group of entities external to the entities resembling. Internal resemblance is a direct relation between the resembling things, which requires, logically, no other object for its possibility. Two shades of color cannot resemble in being both liked by Mary if there were no such person as Mary. But they may resemble internally, directly, independently of the existence or nonexistence of any other object. Clearly, internal resemblance is both the primary and ordinary sense of resemblance. To say that a resembles b in that both are related by R to c is either to say merely that a is related by R to c and b is related by R to c, or to say that the relation of a to c resembles, or is the same as, the relation of b to c. If the former, then the statement about a, b, and c is not a resemblance-statement at all. If the latter, then the statement asserts the internal resemblance between one instance of a relation and another instance of a relation. In neither case is there an irreducible reference to an external resemblance.

Nor is the simplicity of certain qualities incompatible with another fact about them, namely, that even in their intrinsic nature they can be described with more than

6. G. E. Moore, *Some Main Problems of Philosophy*, p. 332; the distinction is discussed on pp. 331-32.

one predicate. A certain simple quality of an individual may be described as pink, red, or color. And there is a sense in which one may speak of the several characteristics of such a simple quality, namely, the characteristics of being pink, being red, and being a color. Obviously, these are characteristics of the nature of the quality, and not merely certain relations of the quality to external objects, such as the relation of being liked by Mary. Yet, although a specific shade of red does have such characteristics in virtue of its intrinsic nature, it may still be simple. How is this possible? The reason is that such characteristics as being pink, being red, and being a color are not logically distinct. They constitute a series in which they are arranged in respect to generality. And the less general characteristic is not, so to speak, outside of the more general, but represents a necessary specification of the latter, with which it can be said to be in a sense identical. Being pink is not related to being red in the way in which being pink is related to being five feet long. To be pink is also to be red, and to be red is to be one of a certain determinate range of specific shades of which pink is a member by logical necessity. The relations of such characteristics of simple qualities will be discussed in detail in Chapter Four. It is sufficient for my purposes here to point out that if the internal characteristics of a simple quality are not logically distinct or independent, then their multiplicity is no threat to the simplicity of the quality. And that it is not a threat to the claim that the affirmation of intrinsic resemblance of two simple qualities requires no specification of the respect of the resemblance should be obvious. For resemblance in respect to being pink is the same as resemblance in respect to being red, or being a color.

Let us now consider the claim that even if there were no complexity in the objects whose resemblance is affirmed, the mere affirmation of their resemblance remains uninformative. For how would the person making it explain what is meant by such an affirmation? The only possible way to explain this is to indicate the general words which are applicable to the terms of the resemblance. Now this is a curious claim. It amounts to the rhetorical question, "What could 'p' possibly mean but that q?" The strength of this question is that it is used precisely with regard to statements for which there is no statement r such that the reply could be " 'p' means that r." And once it is demonstrated or correctly assumed that there is no such r, it is thought that it has also been demonstrated that "p" could only mean that q. But this whole type of argument is fallacious. For one does not have to find an r which would be what "p" means in order to show that "p" does not mean that q. One can simply say that "p" means that p and nothing else, that in fact "p" could not mean anything else if it is "p" and not some other statement. The Nominalist Theory itself has used this kind of rebuttal of such an argument in defending its claim that to say that certain things are blue is not to say that they have a common quality or that they resemble, but simply that they are blue. And the present claim of the Nominalist Theory can be rejected in the same way. It is not at all obvious that if we say that two things resemble one another we should be able to translate this statement into some other statement. And if we cannot do so, it would not at all follow that the statement really means that the two things can be correctly described with one and the same general word. On the contrary, what might follow is that the statement means just what it says and nothing else, that to say that two things resemble one another is exactly to say that they resemble one another and nothing more or less.

Nevertheless, there is one way in which the above claim could still be substantiated. One can attempt to show that the criteria for the use of the word "resemblance" are such that the only evidence that the word has been used correctly in a certain situation is the ability of the speaker to indicate a certain general word or a description which is applicable to both of the resembling objects. If this could be shown, then there would be every reason for regarding as identical the fact of the resemblance (or recurrence) of certain qualities of two or more objects and the fact that a certain general word is applicable to such objects (or to their qualities). But this cannot be shown, for it is false. A child frequently learns to assert correctly that certain things are like certain other things before he learns the appropriate general words with which he can describe the objects whose resemblance he asserts. We are often struck by the likenesses between different persons' faces and usually are quite unable to classify the aspect of the facial expression of one person which is like a certain aspect of the facial expression of another person. And there are innumerable situations in which the resemblance of certain colors and shapes must be judged, where there can be no question of appeal to the applicability of certain general words to such colors and shapes. Whether a certain shade of red is more like a certain second shade of red than it is like a certain third shade of red is often an important question in painting, interior decoration, the textile industry, and a woman's choice of an evening's attire. To depend for an answer to this question on the fact that such shades might be described with certain general words is usually futile. Where fine discrimination between greater and lesser resemblances is needed, such an appeal is useless. Yet the success or failure of such discrimination is subject to objective, interpersonal scrutiny. It is not at all a matter of subjective impression. Of course, such scrutiny is possible only on the basis of common, objective criteria of the application of the word "resemblance." But what determines whether these criteria are met or not is not the applicability or inapplicability of certain general words to the objects resembling, but the results of our examination of the facts about the situation. But what are these facts? Can one state what these facts are except by stating that certain general words are applicable to certain objects? And if one refuses to state what these facts are, then isn't the whole question put beyond discourse and thus beyond thought? But we have seen that there is a third alternative. One *can* state the facts which are so examined. One can state them by saying that the objects resemble each other.[7]

7. In Chapter Three we shall see that statements of the form "*x* resembles *y*" are incomplete, but for reasons quite different from those given by the Nominalist Theory. In the present chapter I am not concerned with resemblance as such but with the recurrence of qualities. I have used the language of resemblances, instead of the neutral language of recurrences, because the second nominalist argument is usually stated in the former.

5. The Distinction Between Individual
Things and Their Qualities

Is the distinction between individual things and their qualities itself legitimate? And does not the very fact that in stating the problem of universals as that of the proper description of the recurrence of qualities we distinguish between objects and their qualities (e.g., between a hat and its color), and that we speak of the relationship of certain qualities of objects already imply that we have accepted the Identity Theory? For is not the problem precisely whether one can distinguish between an object and its qualities, whether one ought to talk about qualities at all, whether one ought to talk about the book as being blue, whether *there are* qualities? Much of the recent literature on the problem of universals has been concerned with just these questions. And we seem here to be brushing them aside.

It has been widely assumed (1) that to talk about the qualities of objects is to talk about common qualities or universals, and (2) that to talk about common qualities or universals is to accept the existence of such common qualities or universals. The second assumption has received much more attention recently than the first. And there have been at least two theories which attempt to avoid the consequences of the second assumption. Both theories have been regarded as nominalist, and although they are very different from what I have called the Nominalist Theory they should be considered here briefly. According to the first theory, only the use of abstract singular words or apparent names of universals (e.g., "the color red," "wisdom," "felinity") commits us to the existence of universals; and the theory holds (1) that all statements in which such words are used can be translated into equivalent statements wherein such words do not occur but the corresponding general words occur as predicates, and (2) that general words which occur as predicates, though meaningful, are not names, i.e., they do not refer, and thus their use does not commit us to the existence of any entities.[8] According to the second theory, the use of both abstract singular words or apparent names of universals *and* general words commits us to the existence of universals; and it holds that even statements which contain general words used as predicates can be translated into statements containing only names of particular objects, forms of the verb "to resemble," and the phrase "as closely as." [9] For instance, the first theory would attempt to translate the statement "Blue is a color" into "Whatever is blue is also colored" and will hold that the predicates in this latter statement are not names. The second theory, however, refuses to allow that one should simply assume that general words are not names and insists that even statements such as "*a* is blue" must be translatable into statements that entirely avoid the use of general words. It will suggest, perhaps, that the statement "*a* is blue" can be translated into "*a* resembles *b, c,* and *d* at least as closely as *b, c,* and *d* resemble each other," where *b, c,* and *d* are the exemplars of the meaning of the word "blue."

8. Cf. W. V. O. Quine, *From a Logical Point of View;* also, with Nelson Goodman, "Steps toward a Constructive Nominalism," *Journal of Symbolic Logic,* 1947. But see also Quine's *Word and Object,* p. 267.
9. The best exposition of the theory can be found in H. H. Price, *Thinking and Experience,* Chapter 1.

The success or failure of such proposed translations is obviously of considerable philosophical interest. There have been many criticisms of such translations of particular statements and many examples of statements about the translatability of which there are serious doubts.[10] But I shall not dwell on this problem. For I shall argue that even if such translationist programs are successfully carried out, their success would not have the slightest tendency to show that there are not universals and would cast little doubt on the legitimacy of the distinction between individual things and their qualities.

The fact is that nominalistic worries about statements such as "This book is blue" are not due to the implied distinction between the book and its color; they are due to the natural (but not necessarily justified) tendency to *interpret* this distinction as one between a particular and a universal. But, surely, to reject such an interpretation is not at all to reject the distinction between the book and its color. Rather, it is to reject the further statement that the color of the book can also be the color of some other object, e.g., the fountain pen. And it is the question of the truth of such statements as the latter that constitutes the problem of universals. As to the distinction between a book and its color, to reject it is, in addition to being unnecessary to Nominalism and to the Resemblance Theory, also to deny an obvi-

10. For a criticism of the first theory, see Arthur Pap, "Nominalism, Empiricism, and Universals I," *Philosophical Quarterly*, 1959. For a criticism of the second theory, which is especially concerned with H. H. Price's account of it in *Thinking and Experience*, see D. D. Raphael, "Universals, Resemblance, and Identity," *Proceedings of the Aristotelian Society*, 1954-55.

ous fact and to imply an absurd conception of the
nature of individual things. The color of the book is
clearly at least as distinct an object of perception as the
book itself, regardless of whether we consider the book
as a mere collection of qualities or as something to
which qualities "belong." If anything, it is more difficult
to attend to the book and not to its color than it is to
attend to its color and not to the book. And just as one
can consider the spatial relations of the book to certain
other objects, e.g., the fountain pen, so can one consider
the relations of the color of the book to the color of
some other object, e.g., the color of the fountain pen.
To suppose that there are not qualities is to suppose
that individual things have a nature which they obviously do not have and which they cannot be meaningfully said to have.[11]

Consider a statement such as "Orange is more like
yellow than it is like bluè." The first translationist
theory assumes that there are only two possible interpre-
tations of this statement. It may be taken as it stands, in
which case it is supposed to "commit" us to the existence of at least three universals, namely, the colors
orange, yellow, and blue. Or it may be translated into
"For every x, y, and z, if x is orange, and y is yellow, and
z is blue, then x is more like y than x is like z," in which
case, assuming that predicates are not names, we need
be committed only to the existence of individuals, and
not to the existence of colors. Let us ignore the intrinsic

11. Of course, that there is a distinction between individual things
and their qualities, and that there are qualities, does not entail (1)
that qualities can exist separately from individual things, or even (2)
that qualities can be identified independently of the individual things
which they characterize.

difficulties of this translation, such as that if it is to be
at all adequate, "more like" and "is like" should be replaced with, respectively, "more like in color" and "is
like in color," a revision that may only cause difficulties
for the theory. I suggest now that there is a third interpretation of the above statement, which in fact is the
natural one and is neutral with respect to the dispute
between "realism" and "nominalism." We can take the
statement *as it stands* and understand it as committing
us, if to anything at all, only to the existence of blue
color-qualities, yellow color-qualities, and orange color-
qualities of individual things. (A similar interpretation
can be given to other problematic statements. For example, "Mary's favorite color is pink" surely means neither
that there is a universal color pink that is the object of
Mary's favors, nor that Mary's favorite individual things
are pink, but that of all color-qualities of individual
things the pink ones are Mary's favorites.) An "onto-
logical commitment" to the existence of such qualities
is not nominalistic because it does not include a commitment to their particularity. But neither is it realistic,
for it does not include a commitment to the universality
of the qualities. And it is not a commitment to the
existence of color-qualities which may be, say, blue in a
nonreferring sense of "blue." For the sense in which a
color-quality *is* blue is not the sense in which a book *is*
blue; it is more like, though not the same as, the sense
in which John's wife *is* Peter's sister.

It seems, therefore, that the success or failure of the
first translationist theory would be irrelevant to the
question whether there are universals. But is it not relevant to the question whether there are qualities? If suc-

cessful, surely it would show that reference to qualities, be they particular or universal, is not required for the assertion of any fact. Let us ignore our doubts about the nonreferring role of general terms, and suppose that it would. Yet, interesting though this would be, I doubt that anyone should wish to conclude from it that there are not, or that there is less evidence for supposing that there are, qualities. Our ability to state every fact we wish to state without committing ourselves to the existence of universals might have been important, for in general we suppose that the existence of universals is suspect and we wish to avoid expressions that seem to force us to accept it. But, surely, there is nothing philosophically suspect, undesirable, or at all doubtful about the existence of qualities of individuals, even if it were undesirable that we describe such qualities as universals. It is true that we do not ordinarily assert the existence of qualities of individual things, and perhaps it is true that we can translate all statements that entail such assertions into statements that do not. But even if, following Aristotle, we say that in its primary sense "existence" is applicable to individual things, we should certainly not deny to ourselves the right to assert also the existence of the qualities of individuals, though in a secondary sense of "existence." In a tertiary sense of "existence" we may have the right to say that the color blue exists even if there are not any blue things, as long as it is possible that there be blue things.[12]

The same defect is found also in the second translationist theory, which attempts to translate statements

12. See below, section 18.

containing both abstract singular *and* general words into statements containing only names of individuals, forms of the verb "to resemble," and an expression such as "as closely as." As in the case of the first theory, the supposition that the success of such a translation would show that there are not universals rests on the mistaken assumption that the use of general words commits us to the existence of universal qualities. But there is no reason for making this assumption. If the use of general words commits us to the existence of anything, it commits us to the existence of qualities. But whether these qualities are universal or particular is a question that must be decided independently, and the success of the translationist program would not have the slightest tendency to contribute to such a decision. If the use of the word "blue" in the statement "My fountain pen is blue" commits me to the existence of something, surely it commits me only to the existence of my fountain pen's blue color-quality. If the latter is identical with all other blue color-qualities, as the Identity Theory would claim, then the use of the word "blue" might commit me to the existence of a universal. But if it is a distinct particular quality which only resembles all other blue color-qualities to a specified degree, then the use of the word "blue" would not commit me to the existence of a universal. It should not be objected here that the use of a general word cannot commit us to the existence of a *particular* quality because it applies to more than one individual thing. If the Resemblance Theory of the applicability of general words is true, then the fact that a general word can apply to more than one thing would be explained by the resemblance of certain *particular* qualities of the things to which it applies.

Again, as in the case of the first translationist theory, it could also be argued that the program of the second theory is relevant to the problem of universals because if successful it would show that no reference to qualities, be they universal or particular, is ever necessary in language. To be able to show this would be extremely important. But I don't think that its importance would consist in a solution of the problem of universals. For, even if one could assume that if we can say everything without referring to universals then we would have no other reason for supposing that universals exist (an assumption that both translationist theories rather uncritically make), it still would not follow that if we can say everything without referring to qualities then we would have no reason for supposing that qualities exist. Surely we have many other reasons for distinguishing between an individual thing and its qualities and for asserting that both exist, though perhaps in different senses of "existence." The success of the second translationist theory would demonstrate an important fact about language. But it is unthinkable that it would demonstrate that there are not qualities. And to attempt to demonstrate this by appealing to some principle of conceptual parsimony would be to confuse economy with miserliness.

6. *The Problem of Universals Explained*
with Reference to a Concrete Instance

I have reached the conclusion that, contrary to the thesis of the Nominalist Theory, the fact of the recurrence of a certain quality is neither identical with, nor logically dependent upon, the fact that a certain general word is applicable to certain objects. Does it follow that the problem of the correct description of the recurrence of qualities is a problem about the nature of the world, that its solutions may constitute parts of our knowledge of the world? It is with this question that I shall be concerned in the present chapter. First, I shall attempt to state the problem of universals, in so far as it is concerned with the description of the recurrence of qualities, by describing a concrete instance of it. Second, I shall consider whether the usual descriptions of the recurrence of a quality have cognitive significance in the traditional sense that either (1) one of them is literally true and the other false, or (2) while both are true, they suggest different theories about the fact which they describe, one of which theories is literally true and the other false. Third, I shall examine in detail certain reasons that G. F. Stout and G. E. Moore have given for their preferences for certain descriptions of the recurrence of qualities, with the hope that such an examination may disclose more clearly the nature of the disagreement between the different theories about the correct description of the recurrence of qualities. Fourth, I shall consider the possibility that the cognitive significance of the problem of universals does not consist in the actual truth or falsehood of certain descriptions of the recurrence of qualities but in the illuminating nature of the reasons which a philosopher gives in support of his preference for some of these descriptions.

Let us consider a rectangular sheet of paper which has the following characteristics. The sheet is divided into four regions by three vertical lines, one of which passes through the center and the other two respectively to the left and to the right of it at equal distances. I shall refer to the region at the extreme left as region 1, to the region next to it as 2, to the region immediately to the right of 2 as 3, and to the region at the extreme right as 4. Region 1 is uniformly red, 2 is uniformly yellow, 3 is uniformly red but not the same shade of red as that of 1, and 4 is uniformly the same shade of red as that of region 1. Now if for some reason we are asked to describe this sheet of paper in as much detail as possible, we may make a number of true statements about it such as the following: "The sheet is divided into four distinguishable regions," "Region 1 is uniformly red," "Each region is a rectangle," "The sheet is now resting

on the surface of the table in my study," "Region 4 is to
the right of region 2," "The color of region 1 is more
like the color of region 4 than like the color of region
3." Among the many possible statements about our
object of study there would be four which are of particular interest to us:

P: "The color of region 1 and the color of region 3 resemble each other, though not exactly."

Q: "The color of region 1 and the color of region 3 are
one and the same general color."

R: "The color of region 1 and the color of region 4 resemble each other exactly."

S: "The color of region 1 and the color of region 4 are
one and the same."

There is no reason for supposing that we could not also
give proper names to the sheet of paper and to all the
distinguishable elements in it, i.e., the regions and their
colors. For instance, the color of 1 can be given the name
"a," the color of 2, the name "b," the color of 3, the name
"c," and the color of 4, the name "d." The designatum
of such a name would be simply the color of the respective region in so far as that color is distinguishable from
the region which it occupies. Whether such a designatum is a particular or a universal is a question which
is subsequent to the identification of the designatum;
for the designatum of such a name is identified simply
by reference to the surface region which it occupies.
Therefore, no commitment is made to any theory of
universals in distinguishing the colors of the regions
from the regions they occupy and in speaking of the
colors as four colors; for we identify each color only by
reference to the region it occupies and thus there are

four colors that are so identifiable. But if we say that they are four, are we not committing ourselves to the particularity of the qualities of individual things? We are not. The fact that one can identify a quality by reference to the thing to which it belongs and thus distinguish it from a similar quality which is identified by reference to its belonging to another thing is the raw fact with which the problem of universals is concerned. Perhaps the assertion that the two qualities are one quality is a false description of this fact. But it is not a logical mistake. For the problem of universals is precisely this: whether there are cases in which one can speak of two qualities as being one quality without committing simply a logical mistake. To say that the very fact that the color of 1 and the color of 4 are identifiable in different ways (the color of 1 by reference to its occupancy of region 1 and the color of 4 by reference to its occupancy of region 4) already entails that they are different and therefore not one and the same color, is simply to reject the *possibility* of there being cases in which one can properly speak of two qualities as being one; and to reject this possibility is simply to accept a particular solution of the problem of universals.

Now what is philosophically interesting about statements P, Q, R, and S is that they naturally fall into pairs: (P, Q) and (R, S). The reason they do so is that the two statements in each pair seem to be drawing attention to one and the same fact about the sheet of paper, and, if made in a situation in which no philosophical considerations would be relevant, both would be regarded as verified or falsified because of one and the same fact. Both statements in each pair appear to convey exactly the same information about the sheet of paper.[1] At the same time, they are not obviously synonymous. While *R* seems to suggest that the color of region 1 and the color of region 4 are distinct colors, though related by resemblance, *S* seems to suggest that they are not distinct colors at all, that in fact they are identical. While *P* seems to suggest that the color of region 1 and the color of region 3 are also distinct, though related by resemblance, *Q* seems to suggest that there is a sense in which they are not distinct, that in a sense they are one and the same color, namely, one and the same general color, though of course they are not one and the same specific color as *S* claims that the color of region 1 and the color of region 4 are.

Are both statements in each pair correct or acceptable? And if they are not, which one of them is the correct or acceptable one? These two questions can be regarded as a concrete instance of the problem of universals. It should be pointed out at the very beginning, however, that the philosophical question of the correctness or acceptability of statements such as *P, Q, R,* and *S,* with which we shall be concerned, is not intended as a question about conventional usage or linguistic etiquette. As we saw in Chapter One, the recurrence of qualities is a fact about the world, and not a fact about language. And the problem of its description is to be understood

1. Sometimes it is said that qualitative identity statements and qualitative resemblance statements cannot be used to describe the same facts, because of the "transitivity of identity" and the "nontransitivity of resemblance." There is some truth in the remark. However, it draws attention not to the fact that resemblance is a nontransitive relation, but to the fact that it cannot be a two-term relation. In Chapter Three I shall examine this question in detail.

as one about the nature of the world; i.e., the purpose
of an attempted solution of it may only be to discover
a certain truth about the world. This is not to say, of
course, that there is such a problem. It may be that the
only possible question about the correctness or acceptability of $P, Q, R,$ and S is one about conventional usage
or linguistic etiquette. But whether this is so or not cannot be merely assumed. It must be shown in detail. And
the purpose of the present chapter is precisely to consider whether the problem of universals is indeed about
the nature of the world, and in what sense it should be
said to be "about the world."

We can now immediately list the possible solutions of
the concrete instance of the problem of universals which
was described above, together with the more obvious
reasons that can be given in support of each solution.

Theory A: Both statements in each pair are correct or
acceptable. For they draw attention to, or describe, one
and the same fact; both are true, and if one were false
the other would also be false.

Theory B: P is correct and Q is incorrect. For the color
of region 1 and the color of region 3 are qualitatively
different. And to say that they are one and the same
general color implies that one can observe some distinct
component in both which is identical; but one cannot
observe such a distinct component.

Theory C: Q is correct and P is incorrect. For there is
no such relation as qualitative resemblance unless it
consists in some kind of identity of the qualities which
are said to resemble each other. And saying that the

color of region 1 and the color of region 3 are one and the same general color does not imply that they have an observably distinct component which is identical in both, in addition to their other components which constitute their differences. The different specific shades of red in the colors of region 1 and region 3 are not components of the colors, nor is their redness another component—the shades are different determinates of the same determinable, they are internal to their redness.

Theory D: R is correct and *S* is incorrect. For the very fact that the color of region 1 and the color of region 4 belong to, or occupy, different regions of the sheet of paper entails that the two colors cannot be one and the same color; if they were one and the same we could not distinguish them and thus we could not even attempt to identify them.

Theory E: S is correct and *R* is incorrect. For while there is a difference between region 1 and region 4, the *color* of region 1 is not different from the *color* of region 4; and to say that the colors resemble each other, even if exactly, is to imply that they are different, which they are not.

There are several preliminary observations to be made about the above five theories. While *A* is inconsistent with any of the remaining four, this is not the case with *B, C, D,* or *E*. In particular, *B* is consistent with either *D* or *E, C* is consistent with either *D* or *E, D* is consistent with either *B* or *C,* and *E* is consistent with either *B* or *C. B* or *D* or both can be referred to as the Resemblance Theory, and *C* or *E* or both can be referred to as the Identity Theory. But we must remember that theories

B and *E* can be held together as components of one and the same theory,[2] and that theories *C* and *D* can also be held together, though it seems unlikely that one would wish to do so. Also, it may be worth mentioning that Theory *A* can be regarded as the conjunction of the theory that statements *P* and *Q* are equally correct (*Ax*) and the theory that statements *R* and *S* are equally correct (*Ay*). *Ax* would be inconsistent only with *B* or *C*, and *Ay* only with *D* or *E*. But it is unlikely that one would wish to claim that only one of the two subdivisions of Theory *A* is true.

The reason for the logical relationships mentioned above is, of course, the important difference between statements *P* and *Q*, on one hand, and statements *R* and *S*, on the other. The sense in which the color of region 1 is said to resemble the color of region 3 is very different from the sense in which the color of region 1 is said to resemble the color of region 4; this is why one would wish ordinarily to specify that the resemblance of the latter is exact, while that of the former is not. The difference between the sense in which the color of region 1 and the color of region 3 can be said to be one and the same and the sense in which the color of region 1 and the color of region 4 can be said to be one and the same is even clearer. Ordinarily it is necessary to specify that the former are one and the same *general color*, though there are cases in which such specification is not required ("She always wears clothes of one and the same color"). In general, the sense in which one can speak of the recurrence of a specific shade of red is different from

2. E.g., by R. I. Aaron, in his *Theory of Universals*.

the sense in which one can speak of the recurrence of
the color red. According to the Resemblance Theory,
the former kind of recurrence is to be described as exact
resemblance, and the latter as inexact resemblance. According to the Identity Theory, the former is to be
described as specific qualitative identity, i.e., as the presence of the same specific universal in the instances of
the recurrent quality, and the latter is to be described
as generic qualitative identity, i.e., as the presence in
the instances of the quality of the same generic (or determinable) universal but not of the same specific (or
determinate) universal.[3] The distinction is of fundamental importance in the theory of universals. As we
shall see, the arguments for and against specific universals are in many respects different from the arguments for and against generic universals. And one may
feel compelled to adopt the Identity Theory with respect
to exact resemblance, but the Resemblance Theory with
respect to inexact resemblance.

Now the purpose of an examination of the problem
of universals is to determine which of the above five
theories are true, and which false. And, clearly, one must
begin with Theory A, for it is inconsistent with each of
the other four. Should we find that Theory A ought to
be accepted, then the remaining four would not need
to be examined at all. Thus the first question is whether

3. Clearly, the notions of specificity and exactness as they are employed in this context are not relative. A quality of one object and a
quality of another object resemble exactly or are specifically identical
if there is no *qualitative* difference between them. It is not self-contradictory to suppose that there are such qualities. Whether in fact there
are such qualities is a matter for empirical inquiry. It seems obvious
that there are.

or not statements P and Q are equally correct, and whether or not statements R and S are equally correct. However, I shall limit the discussion in this chapter to the question whether R and S are equally correct. For if there is a sense in which they are not equally correct, there would be little doubt that in that sense P and Q also would not be equally correct. On the other hand, if we find that there is a sense in which R and S are equally correct, then we can consider whether there is a sense in which only P and Q can be said to be not equally correct.

7. Is One of the Two Theories True and the Other, False?

The argument in support of the view[4] that statements R and S are equally correct or acceptable can be short, simple, and straightforward. Surely the color of region 1 and the color of region 4 are exactly alike. And just as surely they are one and the same color. One can make either statement and still be saying the same thing. No one would understand one of the statements to be saying something which the other one is not saying, except for the mentioned cases of the occasional ambiguity of the phrase "one and the same." No one would use one of the statements in a concrete situation and refuse to allow that the other one could be used just as correctly. Our reasons for accepting one of the statements as true would be exactly the same as our reasons for accepting the other statement as true. The consequences of ac-

4. Cf. H. H. Price, *Thinking and Experience*, Chapter 1; also Nicholas Wolterstorff, "Qualities," *Philosophical Review*, 1960.

cepting one of them are exactly the same as the consequences of accepting the other one, both in science and
in everyday life. In short, our criteria of the correct use
of sentence R are exactly the same as our criteria of the
correct use of sentence S. So what is the problem? There
is no real problem, and the Identity Theory and the
Resemblance Theory are merely alternative ways of describing the same facts.

Yet, however convincing such an argument may seem,
its opponents must be given opportunity to state their
case. Now there would seem to be two traditional ways
in which one can claim that one of statements R and S
is correct or acceptable cognitively, while the other one
is not. First, one can simply assert that one of the two
statements is true, while the other one is false. Second,
one can admit that as used in everyday discourse both
statements are true, but claim that they *suggest* different
theories about the fact which they describe, of which
theories one is true and the other false.

The claim that only one of statements R and S is a
true description of the relationship of the color of region
1 and the color of region 4 is usually supplemented with
the assertion that the other statement, the statement
which is false, is false only if taken literally, and that in
fact it is nothing but a misleading version of the true
statement. Thus the Resemblance Theory would claim
that ordinary discourse about common qualities is *really*
only misleadingly worded discourse about resemblances;
and the Identity Theory would claim that ordinary discourse about resemblances is really only misleadingly
worded discourse about common qualities. The reason
for this supplementary claim which each theory usually

makes is the theorist's natural unwillingness to reject as
false a very large number of statements that everyone,
including the theorist himself in his nonphilosophical
moments, accepts as true. Yet, while we may commend
him for his wish to conform to common sense as far as
his theory will allow him, he must be reminded that
what he considers to be false descriptions of the recurrence of qualities *if* taken literally, must nevertheless be
such that they *can* be taken literally, that they can be
understood as being literally false, even if we could always reinterpret them so that they would be considered
true. For the very possibility of the Identity Theory and
of the Resemblance Theory rests on the possibility of
sharply distinguishing between statements such as *R* and
statements such as *S*. Were such statements not really
different, were they incapable of at least being considered to be so different that one of them is literally
true and the other literally false, neither theory could
claim that its description of the recurrence of qualities
is literally true and that the other theory's description is
literally false.

How would one defend the claim that one of statements *R* and *S* is literally true and the other one false?
The defense seems obvious. Both statements are about
the color of region 1 and the color of region 4. But *R*
asserts the presence of a relation of resemblance between
the color of region 1 and the color of region 4, while *S*
asserts the identity of the two colors, i.e., the presence
of a common quality in regions 1 and 4; and, it would
seem, these are two very different assertions. While we
sometimes speak of identity as a relation, it is not at all
a relation in the sense in which resemblance or being-

to-the-left-of or being-greater-than is said to be a relation.[5] It is better to say that while R asserts the presence of a relation between the color of region 1 and the color of region 4, S really denies that they are related at all for it denies that they are different. The defender of R and the defender of S do not disagree about the color of region 1 or about the color of region 4; what they disagree about, however, is whether the two colors are one color or merely two colors which resemble one another. And this seems to be a disagreement about an empirical fact. Each theorist can claim that it is through observation that he reaches the conclusion that his description of the relationship of the color of region 1 and the color of region 4 is alone true. The Identity Theorist can claim that, when he looks at the multicolored sheet of paper, he *sees* the identity of the color of region 1 and the color of region 4,[6] and that he does not see any relation of resemblance between them. And the Resemblance Theorist can claim that he *sees* the relation of resemblance between the color of region 1 and the color of region 4,[7] and that he does not see their identity. At the same time, they may say that in ordinary discourse both statements are considered true simply because in ordinary discourse we are interested only in matters of practical significance. And the only thing about the colors of region 1 and region 4 that might have practical significance is the sort of colors they are, and not the nature of their relationship; when we say

5. See below, section 10.
6. Cf. R. I. Aaron, *Our Knowledge of Universals.*
7. Cf. John Stuart Mill, *A System of Logic* (New York and London: Harper and Brothers, 1900), Book 1, chapter III, section 11.

in ordinary discourse that the colors are similar or one and the same, we are interested in the sort of colors that they would have to be if they are similar or one and the same, not in their actual relationship.

This argument against the view that statements R and S are equally correct seems quite plausible, perhaps too plausible. It almost makes the problem of universals as simple as the question, is that thing between the two plates on the table an apple or a pear? In fact, however, the argument is involved in grave difficulties. It has already puzzled us with its use of expressions such as "seeing an identity" and "seeing a resemblance." And were we to substitute for these expressions something less unusual, such as "seeing that x and y are one and the same" and "seeing that x and y are exactly alike," we would have lost the principal advantage that the argument has, namely, its analysis of the situation described by R and S into factors, such that the two descriptions of the situation could be regarded as different because they could be regarded as asserting the existence of different factors in the situation described. But the peculiarity of the expressions "seeing an identity" and "seeing a resemblance" is the least difficulty of the theory. For even if one could say that one does see the identity or the exact resemblance of two colors as in some way distinct from the two colors themselves, it is odd that in such a simple situation as our observation of a multicolored sheet of paper we could genuinely disagree as to what we see; since, *ex hypothesi,* our disagreement does not concern the nature of the colors of the several regions, but only their relationship.

The oddness of such a disagreement is significant. It

shows that the disagreement between the Identity
Theory and the Resemblance Theory is not at all
limited to the question of the correct description of
the multicolored sheet of paper. It is not as if the two
theorists simply looked at the sheet of paper and then
discovered that they disagreed about the description of
a certain fact about it. They disagree about the description of this fact because they *already* disagree about *all*
such facts. If one makes the philosophical claim that
one does not see the identity of the colors of region 1
and region 4, but only their relation of resemblance,
one is also making the claim that one does not see how
any colors or shapes or arrangements of distinct objects
or surface regions could be identical, that one does not
and *cannot* see any identity of this sort. And if one
claims that one does not see a relation of exact resemblance between the colors of region 1 and region 4 but
only their identity, one also claims that one does not
and cannot see such a relation in any other situation.
When this peculiarity of the traditional theories of universals becomes obvious, one is tempted to dismiss such
theories by simply saying that their claims are analytic
statements and thus not factual, that they are essentially
unverifiable because no observation will ever be allowed
to count as disconfirming, that each claim is such that
nothing could ever count as a reason against it. But the
temptation to say all these things must be resisted. Saying them had a function to perform when it was perhaps necessary to point out that philosophical claims
are not verifiable in the sense in which scientific or
everyday statements can be said to be verifiable. And it
was important to point out this feature of philosophical

claims. But to say that, therefore, such claims as those of the traditional theorists of universals are nonempirical, nonfactual, noncognitive, is either to say once again that they are not verifiable in the sense in which scientific and everyday statements are said to be verifiable, or to express a sweeping conviction about the nature and limitations of human knowledge, a conviction that must be elaborated and defended in very great detail. For a statement is factual if it asserts what may be a fact in the world and empirical if the fact it asserts is directly or indirectly observable. And it is not self-contradictory to say, in this sense, that a statement is factual and empirical but its truth is not subject to appraisal by future and other persons' observation.

Yet the systematic, necessary character of the claims of the Identity Theory and the Resemblance Theory is a reason for a different kind of objection. What is striking is not so much the fact that each claim is such that it is unverifiable, in the sense that its truth is not subject to appraisal by any future or other persons' observation, but that they are *two* opposing claims about *every* situation of a certain very general and very familiar kind. One of the two claims may still be perfectly true, indeed factually true, in the sense that it is a true description of a certain empirical fact. But, then, how could the theorist who makes this claim also claim to know that the opposing claim is false? If X and Y are conversing and then X suddenly announces that he sees a ghost in the room, while Y claims that it is only a shadow, there is a clear sense in which X's statement may be factually true even if it were not subject to verification in the way in which scientific statements are. But at least X can also claim to know that Y's claim is false, for he knows (presumably) what it is to see a shadow. Now, can the Identity Theorist claim that the Resemblance Theory is false? Can he know what would be the case if there were not universals but only resemblances? And, can the Resemblance Theorist claim that the Identity Theory is false? Can he know what would be the case if there were not resemblances but only universals? The point is that while there are situations which both X and Y would describe as one's seeing a shadow and while there are situations which both would describe as one's seeing a ghost, there are no situations which both of our theorists would describe as the presence of universals or as the presence of resemblances.[8] But then how could the Identity Theorist learn the relevant meaning of the word "resemblance" in order to claim that the Resemblance Theory is false? And how could the Resemblance Theorist learn the relevant meaning of the word "universal" in order to claim that the Identity Theory is false? In every situation with reference to which the Identity Theorist would have learned the use of the word "universal," the Resemblance Theorist would have learned the use of the word "resemblance." Indeed, one of them may see a certain factor in such a situation, while the other may not see it or may see a different factor; one may

8. Could the Identity Theorist reject only exact resemblance and thus have a criterion of resemblance derived from inexact resemblance (i.e., could he not adopt both Theory B and Theory E)? But if one holds such a "mixed" theory of universals, he would do so on the grounds that there are enormous differences between exact and inexact resemblance, and thus he would be especially unable to understand the Resemblance Theorist's claims about exact resemblance by using his own criteria of inexact resemblance.

see the identity of the two qualities, while the other may not see it or may see their relation of resemblance. But whatever the one may see, he has no way of ever finding out what it is that the other one *claims* to see. For there is no relevant situation that the one will describe as a case of identity of qualities which the other one would not describe as a case of resemblance of qualities. And the Identity Theorist could never learn that when the Resemblance Theorist uses the word "resemblance" he does not mean identity. Nor could the Resemblance Theorist ever learn that when the Identity Theorist uses the word "identity" he does not mean exact resemblance. So neither one would ever be able to claim that while his theory is true, the other one's theory is false. But could not the Identity Theorist be a former Resemblance Theorist and thus have a first-hand knowledge of both terminologies? Perhaps he could. But how did *he* ever learn the difference between the two terminologies? Perhaps at a certain point in his philosophical career he suddenly stopped seeing a world of qualitative identities and began seeing a world of resemblances. And now he remembers his past mistake and tries to keep others from making it. But was it *then* a mistake at all? And how does he know that *now* the others are making *that* mistake and not another?

The second argument against the theory that both R and S are correct, is a peculiar one. It does not claim that R and S are not both true. But it points out that, even if they are both true, the terminology used in the one is quite different from the terminology used in the other one. Now this difference in terminology may be significant. For it suggests the possibility that there are different *theories* about the fact which, in everyday situations, is equally well described by R and S. And one of these theories may be true and the other false. But they are reflected in the terminologies of statements R and S, and thus one of the latter might be said to be true and the other false, in a very extended sense of the word "true," namely, the sense in which a statement would be called true or false because the terminology used in it is borrowed from or suggests a theory which is true or false. For instance, the statement "This book is blue" and the statement "The surface of this book reflects light rays which are blue" describe one and the same fact and are equally true. But the former statement suggests the theory that colors are "qualities of the object we see," while the latter suggests the theory that colors are "qualities of light, having its rays for their entire and immediate subject." [9] And if only the latter theory is true, then in an extended sense one could say that the statement "This book is blue" is false. Now what sort of theories could be thus suggested by statements R and S? It would seem that, at the very minimum, any relevant theory about the fact described by R and S would assert the presence in it of certain elements or relations. And a conflicting theory would assert the presence in it of at least one element or relation the absence of which is asserted by the first theory, or the absence of at least one element or relation the presence of which is asserted by the first theory. Or a theory may describe the fact in greater detail than it is described by statement R or S. It may disclose elements

9. *Newton's Philosophy of Nature,* ed. H. S. Thayer (New York: Hafner Publishing Company, 1953) , pp. 77-78.

in this fact which are not disclosed by R or S. It may show that the fact has a certain structure which is not reflected in R or S. It may provide a true or false, adequate or inadequate, analysis of the fact of which both R and S are nevertheless perfectly and equally true descriptions.

But, however comforting such an account of the difference between statements R and S may be, it is not at all helpful. For what sort of theoretical account of the fact described by the statement "The color of region 1 and the color of region 4 are one and the same" and the statement "The color of region 1 and the color of region 4 resemble each other exactly" can be both more illuminating than either one of these statements and yet not simply a statement describing a completely different fact? What elements or relations in this situation can such a theory point out that are not already pointed out in one or both of the above two statements? What details of the situation would a theory disclose which are not already disclosed by one or both of the statements? What complexity in the situation would the theory reflect which is left unreflected in statements R and S? Clearly, none. At most, any relevant theory suggested by the terminology of R (or of S) would be simply a paraphrase of R (or of S). For, regardless of whether or not both R and S are true and correct, there is nothing in the situation described by R and S that has not already been mentioned either in R or in S or in both. Any complexity that one might be able to find in the color of region 1 or in the color of region 4 or in both would seem to be obviously irrelevant to the problem of universals. And even if it made sense to speak of the complexity of the relation of the two colors, still the problem is not what the distinguishable elements in the relation may be, but what the relation as a whole is.

8. What Kind of Reasons Lead One to Accept the One Theory and Reject the Other?

We seem to have reached the conclusion that we cannot accept either one of the two traditional arguments in support of the claim that the difference between alternative descriptions of the recurrence of a quality (e.g., R and S) is a cognitive difference, one that concerns the nature of the world. Both R and S are true. Or, if the multicolored sheet which we are examining were somewhat different, both might be false. But it cannot be the case that one is true and the other false. Nor could there be any profound theoretical analyses of the fact asserted by R and S, one of which might be true and the others false.

Does this mean that Theory A, according to which R and S (and P and Q) are both true and equally correct, is the true theory about the problem of universals? I have assumed throughout this discussion that a philosopher's preference for one of statements R and S can have cognitive significance only if one of these statements is literally true and the other one false, or if they suggest different theories about the structure of the fact they describe, one of which is literally true and the other false. But perhaps this assumption is not justified. For, surely, the nature (cognitive or noncognitive) of a philosopher's preference for one of the statements R and

S can be determined only by reference to the *reasons* he may give for such preference. And there may be cognitively significant reasons for preferring *R* or *S*, other than simply the truth of *R* or *S*. At least such a possibility should not be dismissed without careful consideration. And I shall consider this possibility by examining in detail one reason given by G. F. Stout for rejecting the Identity Theory and one reason given by G. E. Moore in defense of the Identity Theory.

Stout's argument runs as follows. "This whole doctrine . . . of the singleness of characters, whether qualities or relations, seems to me fundamentally wrong. A character characterizing a concrete thing or individual is as particular as the thing or individual which it characterizes. Of two billiard balls, each has its own particular roundness separate and distinct from that of the other, just as the billiard balls themselves are distinct and separate. As Jones is separate and distinct from Robinson, so the particular happiness of Jones is separate and distinct from that of Robinson." [10] What exactly is the argument? One may restate it as follows. The local separation of two objects (e.g., two billiard balls, or Jones and Robinson, or region 1 and region 4 of our sheet of paper) entails the local separation of their respective characters (or qualities), e.g., roundness, happiness, color. But the local separation of two objects entails their nonidentity. Therefore, the local separation of the characters of two objects entails the nonidentity of these characters. In other words, assuming that he has proved that the color of region 1 and the color of

10. G. F. Stout, *The Nature of Universals and Propositions*, p. 4.

region 4 are locally separate by inferring this from the local separation of regions 1 and 4, Stout's claim is that if the local separation of two objects entails their non-identity, then the local separation of two colors should also entail their nonidentity.

And how does G. E. Moore reject this reason for abandoning the Identity Theory? He distinguishes between the sense in which two *things* (material objects and presumably also objects such as our regions 1 and 4) can be said to be locally separate and the sense in which two qualities (e.g., the color of region 1 and the color of region 4) can be said to be locally separate. And then Moore admits that the local separation of things (or regions) does entail their nonidentity, but denies that the local separation of qualities entails their nonidentity. For, according to him, the local separation of two qualities is nothing but the fact that one quality belongs to a concrete thing which is locally separate (in the sense of "local separation" in which *things* are said to be locally separate) from a concrete thing to which the other quality belongs. And Moore concludes that "with *this* sense of 'locally separate,' it seems to me perfectly obvious that a quality can be 'locally separate' from itself: one and the same quality *can* be in two different places at the same time." [11] In other words, Moore accepts Stout's premises that (1) the local separation of things entails their nonidentity and that (2) the local separation of things entails the local separation of their respective qualities. But he refuses to accept Stout's claim that if the local separation of two *things* entails their

11. G. E. Moore, "Are the Characteristics of Particular Things Universal or Particular," in *Philosophical Papers*, p. 25.

nonidentity then the local separation of two *qualities* should also entail their nonidentity.

What is exactly the basis of this disagreement between Stout and Moore? I think that it is fair to describe it in the following way. Stout applies the same criteria of identity to qualities, such as colors, that are applied in everyday discourse to individual things; in particular, he so applies the criterion from location in space, according to which local separation is a sufficient condition of nonidentity. Moore, on the other hand, refuses to apply to qualities some of the standard criteria of identity for individual things; in particular, he refuses to apply to qualities the criterion from location in space. Stout refuses to speak, say, of the color of region 1 and the color of region 4 as being one and the same color, solely on the ground that the two colors are locally separate. And Moore insists that speaking in this way is perfectly proper. But each one thinks that he can prove his case, and certainly does not suggest that the disagreement is merely one of blind preference for a particular terminology. Stout's proof is based on his (implicit) claim that the sense in which two individual things are said to be locally separate is sufficiently similar to the sense in which qualities (such as colors) are said to be locally separate in order to justify drawing the same sort of conclusion from each assertion: that the things are not one and the same object, and that the qualities are not one and the same quality. Moore's proof, on the other hand, is based on his (explicit) claim that the sense in which two individual things are said to be locally separate is not sufficiently similar to the sense in which qualities are said to be locally separate in order to justify

drawing from the latter assertion the same sort of conclusion that one can draw from the former: that the
locally separate entities are not one and the same entity.
So the disagreement between Stout and Moore on the
problem of universals seems to be, at least for the arguments considered here, primarily one about the sense
of the expression "local separation" or any of the latter's
equivalents in everyday discourse. According to Stout,
when used with respect to qualities this expression is
used in the same way it is used with respect to individual
things. According to Moore, when used with respect to
qualities this expression is used in a very different way
from the way in which it is used with respect to individual things. What sort of disagreement is this? Could
it have cognitive significance, in the sense that one of
the philosophical opponents may have a certain knowledge of the world which the other does not have?

There are several familiar ways in which one can
classify the disagreement between Stout and Moore.
First, one can consider it as a disagreement concerning
the ordinary uses of the expressions "one and the same,"
"local separation," and related expressions. And to resolve it, one can examine the ordinary uses of such expressions and discover that either Moore or Stout or
both are wrong. Second, one can consider it to be not
so much a disagreement *about* the ordinary uses of
certain expressions (for surely neither Stout nor Moore
would have thought that this was what they were dis-
agreeing about), but a disagreement *due* to either
Moore's or Stout's or both Moore's and Stout's uncon-
scious deviations from these uses. And then one can explain these deviations either (1) as systematic, in which

case they constitute new uses that once explained would cause no puzzles, or (2) as sporadic, in which case they do not constitute genuine, real uses at all since, being sporadic, they cannot be governed by objective criteria of correctness. And then one can attempt to resolve the disagreement either, in the first case, by bringing the new uses of the expressions out into the open where they would mislead no one, or, in the second case, by patiently drawing attention to the ordinary uses of the expressions until either Stout or Moore or both recognize their utterances of these expressions as strictly senseless, as determined by no rules. Clearly, if we accept the first way of classifying the disagreement between Moore and Stout, it would have a peculiar kind of cognitive significance: for it would be disagreement about the ordinary uses of certain expressions and presumably to know, or be clear about, the ordinary uses of certain expressions is to know something. Yet it would be knowledge about language, and it is obvious that neither the Identity Theorist nor the Resemblance Theorist is seeking such knowledge; though, if we reach the conclusion that there is no other knowledge that they can have, they should perhaps seek what they can have.

A third explanation of the disagreement between Stout and Moore is based in part on the second. According to it, Moore or Stout or both are using certain expressions such as "one and the same" and "local separation" in new, unusual ways, though their new uses of such expressions are genuine, in the sense that they can be given objective criteria of correctness. But the third explanation goes beyond the second in adding that either Moore or Stout or both are also *advocating* their revision of language, that they are not merely using certain expressions in unusual ways but somehow claiming that these are the ways in which such expressions ought to be used.[12] Thus, it could be pointed out that Stout is advocating a revision (purely theoretical, of course, and hence harmless) of language such that in respect to no situation involving two locally separate individual things, *a* and *b,* would it be correct or proper to say that the color of *a* and the color of *b* are one and the same. And it might be held that Moore is merely pointing out that as a matter of fact it is quite correct to say in certain cases that the color of *a* and the color of *b* are one and the same; so Moore is doing nothing but defending the ordinary uses of certain expressions as against their proposed unusual Stoutian uses.

A fourth explanation of the disagreement between Stout and Moore includes the third but adds that Stout or Moore or both are advocating certain new uses of given expressions *because* they want to emphasize important similarities and differences in the uses of these expressions. For instance, one might hold that Moore is emphasizing the differences between the uses of "one and the same," "local separation," and related expressions with regard to individual things and their uses with regard to qualities, while Stout is emphasizing the similarity of these two sets of uses. Or one might claim that in rejecting the (philosophical) correctness of any statement of the form "the color of *x* and the color of *y* are one and the same," Stout is really, and perhaps valuably, illuminatingly, emphasizing the dissimilarity be-

12. Cf. Morris Lazerowitz, "The Existence of Universals," *Mind,* 1946.

tween such uses of the more general form "x and y are one and the same" and other uses of this form, e.g., in "The man I saw yesterday and the man I am talking to now are one and the same." On the other hand, Moore, in asserting the correctness of some statements of the form "the color of x and the color of y are one and the same" is really, and perhaps also illuminatingly, valuably, emphasizing the similarity of such a use of the more general form "x and y are one and the same" to its use in the statement "The man I saw yesterday and the man I am talking to now are one and the same."

A fifth account of the disagreement between Stout and Moore includes the main thesis of the fourth account, but adds a thesis peculiar to itself. And this thesis can be stated as follows, though it is never given a very clear form. Moore's and Stout's revisions of language or defenses of the ordinary uses of language indeed emphasize similarities and dissimilarities in the uses of certain linguistic expressions which are of special interest to the problem of universals. But this emphasis has a peculiar nature. It is not merely a way of displaying greater insight into the uses of such expressions. Were it that, it would not need to be made in the form of vehement assertions and denials of the propriety of certain uses. For there is no clear reason why one cannot simply point out such similarities and differences, perhaps in the form of extensive examples and illustrations. There would be no reason why Moore and Stout should actually disagree: after all they are making complementary, though essentially different, points. But they do disagree and neither one of the two would accept a truce, such as one the possibility of which is suggested by the view that Moore's and Stout's theories are exaggerated ways of pointing out noticed similarities and differences in the uses of certain expressions. Why? Because the *choice* of the similarities and differences to be emphasized (and Moore's choice is very different from Stout's) is neither arbitrary nor is it dictated by a pure interest in the workings of language. It is rather dictated by the forceful intellectual (or perhaps even emotional) drive to regard situations such as that described by the statement, "The color of region 1 and the color of region 4 are one and the same," in a certain peculiar way, in terms of a certain particular model. The philosopher's particular choice of the similarities and differences to be emphasized is dictated by his conception of the general pattern of the sort of situation to be described. And his emphasis itself strengthens this conception and codifies a way of viewing the world. Such a way of viewing the world is not itself a part of one's knowledge of the world. It is essentially a structural aspect of language, and as such is determined by our choice of language and not by the nature of the world. Yet the world must be viewed in terms of *some* conception of the world's general pattern; and, in a sense, the *form* at least of our knowledge of the world is determined by our choice of such a conception. For it is such a conception that makes the world a meaningful whole and thus determines the starting-point, the direction, the goal, and the strategy of our knowledge of the world. What would be some such models, in terms of which general conceptions of the world are born, that lie in the basis of the several theories of universals? One may mention the conception of the world as the shadowy, confused, and turbulent reflection of that which in itself has clarity, order, and stability; or as the totality of points formed exclusively by the meeting of a myriad of inter-crossing lines that are independent of, and go far be-yond, the points which they form; or as the totality of points each of which is connected with every other by a straight line; or as a grand pyramidal hierarchy, each element of which is subsumed under a higher one until the highest provides the whole with order and signifi-cance; or as the development of the definite from the indefinite through the progressive determination of the latter in a process of successive birth and decay. These conceptions of the world are not theories of universals. They are not theories at all. They are merely the basic analogies, the original applications of different models upon the world, each one of which would be elaborated, extended, and solidified by a philosophical theory through sweeping theoretical revisions of language that emphasize some similarities and some differences in the uses of certain key expressions and thus present the world in a different light, as possessing a different struc-ture. And in the case of these particular models, which are sometimes as concrete and untheoretical as the re-flection of the sky in the water of a lake or a sheet of paper with pencil marks on it, the philosophical theories which verbalize their use (rather natural or quite forced) for viewing the world as displaying a certain pattern and hence a certain significance are likely to be theories about universals or at least to include such theories.

9. The Cognitive Nature of the Problem of Universals

Such are some possible accounts of the nature of the disagreement between Moore and Stout. They become plausible when we remember our conclusion that disagreement about the correct description of such facts as that described by statements R and S can be neither disagreement as to which one of the alternative statements is true, nor disagreement about certain theories concerning the structure of this fact, each of which is in some way suggested by one of the alternative descriptions of this fact in everyday discourse. Of the five accounts considered, the second and third expressly held that it is not a cognitive disagreement. The first held that it may have some cognitive character as a disagreement about a philological fact. The fourth view perhaps allows for an interpretation of the disagreement as cognitive in the sense that the different emphases on similarities and differences in the uses of certain expressions increase our grasp of the workings of our language. According to the fifth view, the different and conflicting theories of universals modify theoretically the uses of language in such a way as to present the world in the light of different models and thus to present a different conception of the world. But even according to this account the various theories of universals are not cognitively significant in the sense that one of them might be true and the others false; they are not such that one might contain knowledge of the world which the others do not contain; at most, and in a very vague way of speaking, one of them may present a more detailed or more sophisticated or more suggestive model in terms of which the world can be viewed.

But the fourth and fifth accounts already contain the germ of another explanation of the disagreement in the theory of universals, according to which such disagreement is genuinely about the nature of the world and has no special connection with language, even if statements such as R and S are equally correct and true descriptions of one and the same fact.

According to both the fourth and fifth accounts, the philosopher concerned with the problem of universals rejects some perfectly correct descriptions of certain everyday facts in order to emphasize the differences between the uses of certain expressions in these descriptions and the uses of the same expressions in the descriptions of some other facts; or he extends the use of the expressions to situations in which they are not ordinarily used in order to emphasize the similarity of such extended uses to the ordinary uses of the expressions. But to stop here and to pretend that such a function of the theorist of universals is concerned primarily with language is to depend on an artificial and in fact self-contradictory conception of the uses of linguistic expressions. A descriptive linguistic expression is not used in a vacuum. It is essentially connected with the situations in which it is conventionally used and with the objects which compose such situations, especially the objects to which it may be applied. In fact, what makes it a linguistic expression and not merely a series of marks on paper or a series of sounds is precisely its essential connection with the set of situations in which according to convention it may be used, with the set of objects in such situations with regard to which the conventional use of the expression is determined.

To talk about the use of a descriptive linguistic expression is essentially to talk about a class of situations in the world. There is nothing in the nature of the expression or in the fact of its utterance that either determines the sort of situation in which it can be used or constitutes a change in the situation of its use. The use of linguistic expressions is fundamentally different from the use of nails, hammers, and fountain pens. And the failure to perceive the magnitude of this difference is the cause of some mistaken philosophizing about philosophy. The physical nature of an ordinary tool or instrument determines the thing for doing which it can be used and the ways or techniques in which it can be used in order to do this thing. The standard use of nails is determined primarily by the shape and consistency of nails; there are some uses for which, as a matter of physical fact, only a nail would be suitable; and while a nail may have non-standard uses, e.g., one might use it as a paperweight, even these non-standard uses are determined and strictly limited by its physical nature— while one can use a nail as a paperweight, one cannot use it as fuel. This is why there is a sense in which one may say that the uses of nails, hammers, and fountain pens can be objects of inquiry which are distinct from the woods, metals, and pieces of paper that are elements in the actual situations in which nails, hammers, and fountain pens are used, and that the use of nails is distinguishable from the woods and metals on which nails are used. But this is not the case with linguistic expressions. There is nothing in the physical nature of a word (unless it is too long or too difficult to pronounce) that makes it suitable for some purposes and unsuitable for other purposes. There is no theoretical reason why a certain word should not be given any use whatever that a word can have. For the physical nature of a word allows for all possible uses of this word that are possible uses of a word at all. But, then, one should be able to consider the use of an expression in complete abstraction from the expression itself. One should be able to take a variable *x* and then study, inquire into, or describe the different uses that it can be given without any necessity for substituting an actual word for *x*. One should be able to consider the uses of language without considering the uses of any particular expressions. And this should be possible not because in reality there could be linguistic uses without words used, but because it does not matter *what* and *which* words are given such uses. But what then is distinctive about the *use* of a certain linguistic expression? Clearly, it is not the utterability of this particular expression in certain situations, for any other word could be given this use. The fact that expression *a* rather than expression *b* has a certain use is utterly immaterial to that use of language. (Not so with nails: that objects of such shape and such consistency are used for holding two boards together is an essential aspect of that use of nails.) A use of language is simply the use of *some* expression in a certain class of situations. To recognize the use of *a*, to recognize the meaning of *a*, to recognize *a* as a certain particular descriptive *word* is to recognize a certain class of situations. But may it not be just to recognize the conventions, the

logical rules, governing the use of *a*? Yet, what would
these conventions or logical rules be? How would *they*
be recognizable? A convention determining the use of
a word is a convention about the kinds of situation in
which the word may be uttered. And one can know or
understand the conventions or logical rules determining
the use of the expression only if one knows the class of
situations in which the expression may be used.

And now we can see in what sense concerns with language are not concerns with the nature of the world,
and in what sense concerns with language are concerns
with the nature of the world. One is concerned merely
with language in so far as one is concerned with the
particular words that have certain uses of language. But
one is concerned with the nature of the world in so far
as one is concerned with the uses of language themselves.
Which descriptive words are given what uses is a
philological fact, completely distinct from the nature of
the situations in which the words are used. But that
there are such uses of language, that these uses are
logically related in certain ways, and that they bear to
one another certain similarities and differences is a fact
about the world. It is a fact about the ways in which
we group the objects with which we are acquainted,
about the relationships among such groups of objects,
and about the similarities and differences among such
groups of objects. The convention that such and such a
particular expression has such and such a particular use
is ultimately arbitrary; any other expression could do
equally well. But what is not arbitrary is that there is
such a convention at all. For a convention which determines the use of an expression does not merely specify

that this expression is to have such and such a use. It also specifies the use which it arbitrarily gives the expression. And to specify a use of language is to specify a certain class of situations in the world. That there is such a class at all, that it is *possible* to conceive of such a class is what is nonarbitrary.

Consequently, (1) to understand the use of a descriptive expression is to be acquainted with a certain class of situations in the world, (2) to be aware of a logical relationship between the uses of two expressions is to be aware of a necessary relationship between two classes of situations, (3) to consider the extension of the use of an expression as legitimate is to consider the inclusion of one class of situations in another as legitimate, and (4) to consider the limitation of the use of an expression as legitimate is to consider the exclusion of one class of situations from another class as legitimate. To describe the use of a descriptive expression is nothing more or less than to describe a certain class of situations in the world. To describe a necessary relationship between the use of one expression and the use of another expression is nothing more or less than to describe a necessary relationship between one class of situations and another class of situations. To extend the use of an expression is nothing more or less than to regard the members of a certain class of situations as members also of a certain other class of situations. To limit the use of an expression is to regard the members of one class of situations as excluded from a larger class of situations.

Am I claiming that one can give an ultimate, logically complete explanation of the meaning or use of a certain word by describing the class of situations in which it may be used, that one can identify the latter without using the former?[13] I am not. To make such a claim would be to deny a tautology. To identify the class of all actual and possible situations in which a certain word may be used is to apply a word to this class or to all of its members. And there are three alternative ways in which one may do so. The word used for the identification may be the original word whose meaning is to be explained, in which case no explanation has been achieved. Or it may be a synonym of that word, and then again no explanation has been achieved, for we would have the same problem with the explanation of the meaning of the synonym. Finally, the word may not be a synonym of the word whose meaning is to be explained, and in that case the *identification* would either be totally useless or clearly inadequate. On the other hand, the fact that we cannot identify and describe the class of situations in which an expression may be used in abstraction from the use of that or a synonymous expression does not imply that the use of an expression can be identified and described in abstraction from the class of situations in which it may be used. For there is no such thing as the use of an expression unless it is the class of the situations in which it may be used. But what is primary: the class of situations in which the expression may be used or the use of the expression? If by "the use of the expression" is meant the fact that a certain particular expression has such a use, then, clearly, we must say that the class of situations is primary. But if by "the use of the expression" is meant the possible use

13. See above, sections 2, 3, and 4.

of language which has been assigned, through explicit or implicit convention, to that particular expression, then we must say that neither is primary, because there can be no distinction between the class of situations and the use of the expression. It would be a mistake, however, to interpret this answer as nominalistic. The sense in which there can be no distinction between the class of situations in which *some* word may be used and the use of language which such a word would have is simply that any class of situations in the world is a class of situations with reference to which the use of some expression can be determined.

Now, if the above account of the nature of the use of a descriptive linguistic expression is correct, then it becomes absurd to suggest that in emphasizing similarities and differences in the uses of certain expressions such as "one and the same" and "local separation," the philosopher is concerned primarily with words and their uses and not with the world. It is false that one can compare uses of such expressions and yet not compare the situations in which they are used and the objects essential to these situations. Is it not clear, then, that the comparison involved in the emphases on similarities and differences in the uses of certain expressions has cognitive value in a perfectly clear and commonplace sense? For such a comparison is essentially the comparison of certain situations and hence of the objects in these situations. And the results of such a comparison, whether they be assertions of similarity or assertions of dissimilarity, are assertions about the world and hence are true or false, right or wrong. If one were to assert that a certain animal is really a cat, rather than a dog as some other people may have thought, one could be understood to be comparing the use of the word "dog" with regard to this particular animal with its conventional use with regard to certain other animals and to be reaching the conclusion that the two uses are more unlike than the use of the word "cat" with regard to this animal and the conventional use of "cat" with regard to certain other animals would be. But, surely, what is essential in such a comparison is the fact that one is comparing the animal in question and certain other animals and reaching the conclusion that it is less like some of these animals and more like some other of them. And this conclusion is a statement about the world, which is either true or false, and has no special connection with considerations about language. Of course, a case such as the one just described is not an example of the same sort of activity as that in which the philosopher is engaged. It is only analogous to it, and differs from it in many and very important respects. The objects of philosophical comparison are of the highest degree of generality; hence the conclusions reached are not testable in the sense in which scientific (e.g., zoological) statements are testable; and the very generality of such comparison requires that it be expressed in theoretical revisions of language of sweeping proportions and hence of considerable obscurity. But I must not indulge further in this general discussion of language and of philosophy. Its adequacy can be demonstrated only through the analysis of philosophical theories about specific philosophical questions. The discussion in the remainder of this chapter and in Chapters Three and Four could be regarded as an attempt at just such a demonstration.

Now the disagreement between Stout and Moore can be understood in the following way. Stout is emphasizing the difference between the use of the form "x and y are one and the same" in statements such as "The color of a and the color of b are one and the same" and the use of the same form in statements such as "The man I saw yesterday and the man I am talking to now are one and the same." And such emphasis is really an emphasis on the difference between a situation such as one the elements of which are the color of a and the color of b, where the color of a and the color of b are exactly alike or the same (depending on the particular theory of universals we accept) and a and b are locally separate but contemporaneous, and a situation such as one the elements of which are the-man-I-saw-yesterday and the-man-I-am-talking-to-now, where the two are temporally separate and yet constitute events in one and the same life-history (or are said to be identical, in accordance with some other criterion of personal identity). And Stout appeals especially to one such difference: namely, that the colors are locally separate at one and the same time, while the man-I-saw-yesterday and the-man-I-am-talking-to-now can never be locally separate at one and the same time. On the other hand, Moore's position may be understood as follows. He is emphasizing the similarity between the use of the form "x and y are one and the same" in the statement "The color of a and the color of b are one and the same" and its use in the statement "The man I saw yesterday and the man I am talking to now are one and the same." And such an emphasis is really an emphasis on the similarity of the situation the elements of which are the color of a and the color of b, where the color of *a* and the color of *b* are exactly alike or identical, and *a* and *b* are locally separate though contemporaneous, and the situation the elements of which are the-man-I-saw-yesterday and the-man-I-am-talking-to-now, where the two are temporally separate but constitute events in one and the same life-history. And Moore appeals especially to one such similarity, namely, that just as there are no essential differences between the-man-I-saw-yesterday and the-man-I-am-talking-to-now, so there are no essential differences between the color of *a* and the color of *b*. At the same time Moore rejects Stout's main reason for denying the propriety of the ascription of identity to the colors of different objects, namely the local separation of such colors, by distinguishing two senses of the phrase "local separation," namely, the sense in which colors can be said to be locally separate and the sense in which objects can be said to be locally separate. And this distinction is really an emphasis on the differences between colors and the things which have colors, on the differences between qualities and individuals.

We may generalize the above diagnosis of the disagreement between Moore and Stout into a general account of the disagreement between the Identity Theory and the Resemblance Theory. Both theories are concerned with the question of the proper description of a certain kind of situation in the world, namely, what I have called the recurrence of a quality. And the crucial purpose of such a description is to draw attention to the similarity of this kind of situation to some other fundamental kind of situation in the world, to establish and defend an analogy between the two kinds of situation.

According to the Identity Theory, the analogue to the recurrence of qualities is the identity of individual things. And it defends this claim by pointing out that the instances of a recurrent quality are very much like the "designata" of different descriptions of the same individual. Just as the-man-I-saw-yesterday and the-man-I-am-talking-to-now, though distinguishable, constitute an identical individual, because they have the same essential individual characteristics; so, the theory argues, the spatially distinct instances of a recurrent quality, though distinguishable, constitute an identical quality, because they have the same qualitative nature, i.e., the same essential qualitative characteristics. The Resemblance Theory, on the other hand, regards as the analogue to the recurrence of qualities the various relations among contemporaneous but spatially distinct individuals, e.g., the relation of being a member of the same family. And it defends its claim by pointing out that while the instances of a recurrent quality are (or could be) both locally separate and contemporaneous, the "designata" of different descriptions of the same individual cannot be both locally separate and contemporaneous. The Identity Theory sees a recurrent quality as one individual entity pervading, going through, a number of spatially distinct entities, while the Resemblance Theory sees it as a collection of spatially distinct entities joined by a certain relation. But these different ways of "seeing-as" are defended with arguments designed to defend the respective analogy. And these arguments can be evaluated and their conclusions can be accepted or rejected on the same *general* grounds on which we accept or reject any proposition about the facts in the world.

They are in no important, distinctive way arguments about features of language.

The Identity Theory and the Resemblance Theory of universals are theories about certain facts in the world. They are theories (disguised in the form of assertions that a statement such as R or S is true and another false) about the similarities or differences between facts such as the one described by R and S and certain very general other kinds of facts. But which theory then is the true one? Or is either one of them true? They could not be both true, for they are incompatible. But neither does it seem possible merely to look at region 1 and region 4, and then to look at the-man-I-am-talking-to-now and to remember the-man-I-saw yesterday, and find out which theory is the true one. Why is this so? There would seem to be at least two reasons. First, we must distinguish between the correctness of the philosopher's reason for emphasizing a certain similarity or a certain difference between two objects or situations and the correctness of his decision, expressed in his actual philosophical theory, to assert that the similarity between these two situations or objects is greater than the difference between them, or that the difference is greater than the similarity. Clearly, the reasons the Identity and the Resemblance theories have given in support of their respective claims may themselves be perfectly correct. It would seem to be true, for instance, that while color-qualities are locally separate at one and the same time, the events in the life-history of a person are never locally separate at one and the same time; or that just as there are no essential differences between the-man-I-saw-yesterday and the-man-I-am-talking-to-now, so are there no essential differences between the color of *a* and the color of *b*. But while the reasons for the theories may be both correct, in this sense, it does not follow that the theories themselves are correct. For there might be *other* reasons, reflecting hitherto unnoticed similarities and differences in the world. And they might affect our decision as to which similarity is greater. In a sense, the progress of philosophy may be considered to consist in the systematic accumulation of such reasons, which reflect noticed similarities and differences in the world and are expressed in philosophical distinctions, rather than in the succession of philosophical theories. Secondly, at the level of generality at which the philosopher concerned with the problem of universals is operating, a level indicated by the use of such expressions as "one and the same," "resemble," "exist," etc., the established uses of the key expressions are complex and sometimes even the slightest modification of them has far-reaching consequences. For the established uses of such expressions are determined by reference to situations and objects of fundamental importance and great variety, which must be kept in mind before any decision is reached as to the inapplicability of a certain such expression to a certain object or situation. For instance, Moore's distinction of two senses of "local separation" may well be intimately connected with a theory about the relationship between individuals and their qualities. And this theory itself may have its own insight into the nature of the world, and would have to be examined before one can decide whether to accept Moore's distinction. For the similarities and differences to be considered in the evaluation of a philosophical theory such as a theory of universals are fundamental, all-pervasive, extremely complex and interlocking; concentration on only one aspect of such a net of similarities and differences can often lead to assertions which do not accord with the other aspects. This is why, while Moore and Stout, as well as probably every other writer on universals in the history of philosophy, have contributed good reasons both for the theory that situations such as that described by statements R and S are more like the ordinary situations of identity than they are like the ordinary situations of the relatedness of distinct objects, and for the opposite theory, it is possible also that none of these reasons is sufficient. But this should hardly disturb one, if it is in the discovery of such reasons that the genuine worth of the philosopher's activity is to be found.

The Relation of Resemblance
/three

10. The Distinguishing Feature of the Resemblance Theory

The crucial question in the history of the theory of universals has not been whether the Identity Theory or the Resemblance Theory is true, but whether the thesis of the Identity Theory is intelligible. Indeed, it is only in the last few decades that the Resemblance Theory (or, for that matter, the Nominalist Theory) has been understood as a distinctive theory of universals, one that does not consist merely in the rejection of the Identity Theory. Is it legitimate to speak of certain locally separated qualities as identical? Are common qualities possible? Are there entities which can exist at more than one place at the same time? This preoccupation with the intelligibility of the Identity Theory has been the natural consequence of the general assumption that there can be no serious doubt about the intelligibility of the Resemblance Theory, even if the latter is false. The assertion that the shape of one penny and the shape of another penny are one and the same shape may well seem paradoxical. For, as we have seen, it employs criteria of identity that are different in some fundamental respects from the criteria of the identity of individuals, and it is the latter that constitutes our paradigm of identity. But it seems that the assertion that the shape of one penny and the shape of another penny are related by a certain relation, namely, resemblance, appears paradoxical to no one. For it seems to differ in no significant respect from ordinary statements asserting that a certain relation holds between certain distinct objects.

Now, in the light of the conclusions reached in Chapter Two, we can hardly assume either that the Identity Theory is unintelligible or that it is obviously true. The source of the problem of universals is the fact that situations of the recurrence of qualities are in some respects very much like situations of individual identity, but in other respects very much unlike them. They are like them in so far as, at least in the case of exact resemblance, there are no essential qualitative differences between the instances of a recurrent quality. They are unlike them in so far as the instances of a recurrent quality are locally separated at one and the same time. Thus, it seems that even if the recurrence of a quality is not a kind of identity, neither is it very unlike identity. And it is a sufficient merit of the Identity Theory to have pointed this out, just as it is a sufficient merit of the Resemblance Theory to have pointed out that there are also fundamental differences between the recurrence of a quality and the identity of an individual.

But while the dispute *about* the Identity Theory is whether the instances of a recurrent quality are identical or nonidentical, the dispute *between* the Identity Theory and the Resemblance Theory is whether the instances of a recurrent quality are identical or *resembling*. For the rejection of the Identity Theory and acceptance of the Resemblance Theory it is not enough to show that there are good reasons for considering the instances of a recurrent quality nonidentical. It is also necessary to offer an intelligible and distinctive account of their relationship. No theory which fails to account for this relationship can be preferable to the Identity Theory. No reasons for considering the instances of a recurrent quality nonidentical would be better than the reasons for considering them identical if an intelligible account of the fact of the recurrence of the quality is not offered. Now the Resemblance Theory does offer an account of this fact. According to it, the nonidentical instances of a recurrent quality are related by the relation of resemblance. And its insistence that recurrence is a straightforward relation is, as we have seen, its distinguishing feature, that in virtue of which it is a genuine alternative to the Identity Theory. If this account is intelligible, the reasons for accepting the Resemblance Theory would be at least as good as the reasons for accepting the Identity Theory.

How does one determine whether the account which the Resemblance Theory offers of the recurrence of a quality is intelligible? Not in the way in which one may appraise the intelligibility of the account offered by the Identity Theory. The Identity Theory defends its classification of the recurrence of a quality as identity by employing with regard to the instances of a recurrent quality a set of criteria of identity which is significantly

different from the set of criteria of identity employed
with regard to individuals; and the identity of individuals is the paradigm of identity. Consequently, to attack
the intelligibility of the Identity Theory is to claim that
the former criteria are so very different from the latter,
that they cannot be regarded as criteria of identity at all.
But the Resemblance Theory does not attempt to change
the standard criteria of resemblance. It is not as if the
paradigm of resemblance were the resemblance of individuals, and the recurrence of a quality could be described as resemblance only by changing the standard
criteria of resemblance. For the recurrence of qualities,
i.e., qualitative resemblance, is the paradigm of resemblance. The resemblance of individuals can itself be
understood only by reference to the resemblance of
some of the qualities of individuals (or, according to
the Identity Theory, their identity). It is self-contradictory to say that individuals a and b resemble each other
and yet no quality or characteristic of a resembles (or is
the same as) any quality or characteristic of b. On the
other hand, it is quite legitimate to describe the resemblance of a quality of one individual and a quality of
another individual without even considering whether
the two individuals resemble each other. One cannot
speak of the resemblance of two cats unless one is pre-
pared to specify that the color or shape or character of
the one cat resembles the color or shape or character
of the other cat. But one can speak of the resemblance
of the color or shape or character of the one cat and the
color or shape or character of the other cat without
being committed to say anything about the resemblance
or nonresemblance of the two cats. The color of a certain

automobile may resemble the color of the sea even if the automobile does not resemble the sea. It is useless to argue that if a quality of *a* resembles a quality of *b*, then *ipso facto a* resembles *b*. This latter use of "resembles" with regard to individuals, which incidentally is only found in philosophical discourse, is even more clearly dependent for its criteria on the resemblance (or identity) of qualities. To say, in this sense of "resembles," that *a* resembles *b* is nothing more or less than to say that some quality of *a* resembles (or is the same as) some quality of *b*; and while we do have independent criteria of the resemblance of a certain quality of *a* and a certain quality of *b*, our only criterion of this philosophical resemblance of *a* and *b* is the resemblance (or identity) of some of their qualities.

But if qualitative resemblance, i.e., the recurrence of qualities, is the paradigm of resemblance, then it follows that the intelligibility of the Resemblance Theory cannot be rejected with an argument, analogous to that used against the Identity Theory, that the classification of the recurrence of a quality as resemblance involves excessive deviation from the standard criteria of resemblance. How, then, can one reject the Resemblance Theory as unintelligible? It would seem that this can be done in only one way. It can be argued that qualitative resemblance is distinguishable from qualitative identity only in so far as the former is classifiable in a larger class in which the latter is not classifiable, and that the classification of resemblance in that larger class is itself unintelligible, because of fundamental differences between resemblance and the remaining members of the class. If this can be shown, then it will follow that while there is still nothing wrong about regarding situations of the recurrence of qualities as situations of resemblance, situations of resemblance are no longer distinguishable from situations of qualitative identity.

What is the larger class in which resemblance must be classifiable if it is to be distinguishable from qualitative identity? What is the difference between resemblance and qualitative identity? What is the difference between the statement, "*a* and *b* resemble each other," and the statement, "*a* and *b* are one and the same," *a* and *b* being qualities of distinct individuals? We have seen that their difference consists neither (1) in the fact that the one is true and the other false, nor (2) in the fact that the theory suggested by the terminology of the one is true and the theory suggested by the terminology of the other is false, nor (3) in the fact that one represents proper usage and the other does not. It consists in the fact that while the former statement can be *interpreted* as classifying the recurrence of a quality as a relation, like the relations of being-to-the-left-of, giving, preceding, being-taller-than, the latter can be interpreted as classifying the recurrence of a quality as an identity, like the identity of the-man-I-am-talking-to-now and the-man-I-talked-to-yesterday or the identity of the-hat-you-saw-in-the-store and the-hat-I-am-wearing-now. The Identity Theory prefers the latter kind of classification of the recurrence of a quality because it holds that the recurrence of a quality is more like the identity of an individual than it is like an ordinary relation of two or more distinct objects. The Resemblance Theory prefers the former kind of classification because it holds that the recurrence of a quality is more like an ordinary relation of two or more distinct objects than it is like the identity of an individual. Indeed, it would seem that any theory which presents a genuine alternative to the Identity Theory must hold that the recurrence of a quality is a relation. For such an alternative theory must at least claim that the instances of a recurrent quality are distinct, nonidentical entities. And a relational fact is the only kind of fact that is necessarily a fact about two or more distinct entities. Therefore, to be at all distinguishable from the Identity Theory, the Resemblance Theory must regard resemblance as a relation. And if it is shown that resemblance cannot, *in any sense,* be a relation, then it will follow that the Resemblance Theory has failed to present a genuine alternative to the Identity Theory. Therefore, the problem of the intelligibility of the Resemblance Theory is not whether the classification of the recurrence of a quality as resemblance is proper; for the recurrence of qualities constitutes the paradigm of resemblance. It is the question whether the classification of resemblance *as a relation* is proper. And this latter question is not absurd. The paradigms of relatedness are situations such as a's being to the left of b, a's loving b, a's giving b to c, a's helping b. To ask whether resemblance is a relation is to ask whether a's resembling b is sufficiently similar to such situations in order to justify its classification as a relation. And asking this amounts to asking whether and to what extent the use of statements such as "a resembles b" is similar to the use of statements such as "a is to the left of b," "a loves b," "a gives b to c." Only thus can an attempt be made to reject the Resemblance Theory as unin-

telligible without at the same time making the absurd
attempt to reject the terminology of resemblances as
unintelligible. For if resemblance is not a relation, then
it can only be qualitative identity.[1] The third alternative, which was offered by the Nominalist Theory, has
already been found unacceptable.

But is not identity itself a relation? And if it is, does
not the above distinction between the Resemblance
Theory and the Identity Theory collapse? It seems clear
that either identity is not a relation or that it is a rather
peculiar relation which differs in a certain fundamental
respect from all other relations, including the alleged
relation of resemblance. It is essential to the concept of
relation that the terms of a relation be clearly and unequivocally distinct. And it is just this necessary condition of relatedness that identity must fail to satisfy. The
meaning of "identity" is precisely that the entities which
are said to be identical are not clearly and unequivocally distinct. Indeed, if a and b can be said to be identical, they must also be distinguishable; otherwise we can
neither think nor say that they are identical. And it is
because of this fact that it is at all possible to regard
identity as a relation and statements asserting the identity of two objects as statements asserting that a certain
transitive, symmetrical, and totally reflexive dyadic relation holds between them. At the same time, however,
what is asserted of a and b in saying that they are identi-

1. This is why one does not help the Resemblance Theory if one
explains away the peculiarities of the relation of resemblance by saying
that it is not an ordinary relation, or that it is very different from all
other relations, or that it is a unique relation. Cf. H. H. Price, *Thinking
and Experience*, pp. 25-26.

cal is precisely that they are not, or at least not clearly and unequivocally, distinct. Therefore, assuming that the above condition of relatedness is necessary, if the assertion that *a* and *b* are identical is true then their identity is not a relation. But, even if there is a sense (to be found only in philosophical discourse) in which identity can be said to be a relation, on account of the distinguishability of the objects which are said to be identical, this sense would be very different from that in which relations whose terms are not only distinguishable but also regarded as clearly and unequivocally distinct are said to be relations. And as we have seen, unless resemblance is a relation *in this second sense,* it would not be distinguishable from qualitative identity. Therefore, even if identity is a relation, the distinction between the Identity Theory and the Resemblance Theory remains clear. Henceforth I shall use the word "relation" in its second sense.

Now, to consider whether resemblance is a relation is to consider whether it satisfies the standard necessary conditions of relatedness, i.e., whether the use of resemblance-statements satisfies the general necessary conditions of the use of paradigmatic relational statements, such as *"a* is to the left of *b," "a* gives *b* to *c," "a* precedes *b," "a* loves *b."* There seem to be at least three necessary conditions of relatedness. First, a relation must add a certain characteristic to the nature of each of its terms, which the term would not have if it were not related by that particular relation. Second, a relation must have clearly and unequivocally distinct terms. Third, a relation must have a definite, clearly and unequivo-

cally determinable, *number* of terms.[2] The first condition is necessary in order that a group of related objects
may be distinguishable from a group of arbitrarily chosen objects. The second condition determines the most
obvious essential feature of relations: a relation is necessarily a fact about more than one object; for instance, it
is because of this feature that a relation is distinguishable from the fact of the possession by an individual of
a quality or characteristic. The third condition is implied by the first and second. If a relation does not have
a definite, clearly and unequivocally determinable number of terms, then (1) there would be no possibility of
understanding what is the distinctive fact about the
terms which constitutes their relation, and (2) there
would be no possibility of determining that the terms
of the relation are clearly and unequivocally distinct.
Unless we know, in a definite and clear and unequivocal
manner, the number of terms which the relation of giving has, we can neither understand what the relation
of giving is at all nor know that its terms are clearly and
unequivocally distinct.

Does resemblance fail to satisfy one or more of the
above conditions of relatedness? It does not seem possible to claim that it fails to satisfy the first condition.
Whatever resemblance may be, there is an obvious and
clear difference between a group of resembling objects
and a group of arbitrarily selected objects. At least some
kinds of resemblance-statements are quite obviously informative and not at all equivalent in their use to the
mere listing of the objects that are said to resemble

2. I.e., a relation, as a logical category, must be describable as *n*-adic,
where *n* is a certain definite number.

each other. Some defenders of the Identity Theory have argued that resemblance (or at least exact resemblance) does not satisfy the second condition, i.e., that it does not have clearly and unequivocally distinct terms. But they have supported their claim by merely assuming that resembling qualities are identical, and thus their defense of the Identity Theory has been circular. In general, it does not seem possible to argue plausibly that the objects which are said to be resembling are not clearly and unequivocally distinct unless one supports such a claim by appealing to the Identity Theory. But does resemblance satisfy the third necessary condition of relatedness? Does it have a definite, clearly and unequivocally determinable number of terms? I shall argue that it does not.

11. The Terms of a Relation of Resemblance

The virtue of the Resemblance Theory is that the relation of resemblance seems to be an ordinary dyadic relation, i.e., one such that the assertion that it holds between certain two objects is logically complete, very much like relations such as preceding, loving, being-taller-than, being-the-square-of, attracting, belonging-to, being-far-from. The typical form of a statement about resemblance is "*x* resembles *y*." Other forms of resemblance-statements, e.g., "*x* is like *y*," "there is similarity between *x* and *y*," "*x* is similar to *y*," "*x* and *y* are alike," are easily reducible to that primary form. Of course, there are singular resemblance-statements which assert the resemblance of more than two objects, such as statements of the forms "x, y, and z resemble each other" and "x resembles y and z." The relation of resemblance in such statements, however, still appears to be dyadic, each statement being readily analyzable as a conjunction of several statements of the primary form "x resembles y." For instance, "a resembles b and c" is equivalent to "a resembles b, and a resembles c," and "a, b, and c resemble each other" is equivalent to "a resembles b, a resembles c, and b resembles c."

Some dyadic relations admit of comparison in degree with another instance of the same relation. For instance, such are the relations of loving, being-far-from, helping, being-interesting-to, perhaps also belonging-to and attracting. Let us call such relations comparative. The typical statement in which the comparative nature of a relation is made clear would have the form "xRy more than wRz," in which w would often be identical with x. The test of the comparative nature of a relation R is whether a statement of the form "xRy more than wRz" is meaningful. The relations I have just mentioned are comparative because the following statements are meaningful: "a loves b more than c loves d," "a is farther from b than c is from d," "a helps b more than c helps d," "a is more interesting to b than c is to d," perhaps also "a attracts b more than c attracts d" and "a belongs to b more than c belongs to d." On the other hand, being-the-square-of, being-taller-than, and being-the-father-of are not comparative relations because ordinarily the following statements would not be meaningful: "a is the square of b more than c is the square of d," "a is taller than b more than c is taller than d," "a is the father of b more than c is the father of d." The distinction between comparative and noncomparative relations is analogous to the distinction between properties or states which admit of variation in degree or quantity, e.g., warm, grey, small, hard, expensive, and properties which do not, e.g., made-of-wood, rectangular, being-six-in-number, excellent. Clearly, the relation of resemblance is a comparative relation. It is possible to make statements of the form "x resembles y more than w resembles z." It has usually been taken for granted that resemblances can vary in degree, just as loves and hardnesses can.

It is characteristic of almost all comparative relations that while it is logically *possible* for any instance of such a relation to be compared in degree with another instance of the same relation, such comparison is not logically *necessary*. Given such a comparative relation R, it is logically possible for its instance in situation aRb to be compared in degree with its instance in situation aRc or situation cRd; but it is not essential to it, it is not logically necessary for the correct description of aRb, that such comparison be made. The statement "aRb" is compatible with the statement "aRb more than cRd," the latter being meaningful. But "aRb" does not entail some statement such as "aRb more than cRd," i.e., a statement such as the latter is not its necessary condition. John's love for Mary can always be compared in degree with John's love for Jane or with Bill's love for Jane; but John can love Mary without loving her more or less or as much as he loves any one else or as some one else loves any one else. If you were to say "John loves Mary" and I were to ask, "More than whom does he love her?", you could either answer my question by saying, "He loves her more than he (or Bill) loves Jane" or simply point out that in saying that John loves Mary you were not committing yourself to being able to say that he loves her more than he loves some one else. And the reason for this is that John's love for Mary is a fact perfectly intelligible in abstraction from any other facts. It is logically possible that there be a world in which the only individuals existing are John and Mary. Even with regard to such a world the statement "John loves Mary" will neither be superfluous nor unintelligible nor uninformative. It makes sense to say that John loves Mary even if no one else loves any one.

However, there seems to be a very small number of comparative relations for which comparison is not only logically possible but also logically necessary. This does not mean that asserting an instance of such a relation intelligibly is impossible unless a comparison of it with another instance of the same relation is also being explicitly made. What is meant is that a statement about an instance of such a relation can be made legitimately only on the assumption that a comparison of it with another instance of the same relation constitutes the context of the statement and can be made explicit on request. Consider the relation being-far-from. Clearly a statement of the form "x is far from y" can occur alone and be perfectly intelligible. But, unless the context makes clear both that a comparison is intended and what the other term of this comparison is, the statement would be essentially incomplete; it would not be possible to determine in what cases it would be true and in what cases false. Suppose that you were to say "Washington is far from New York," and I were to ask you, "It is farther from New York than it is from where?" Clearly, in this case my question must be answered, for otherwise your statement would be vacuous. (Is Tokyo far from New York? Not in the context of space travel.) In fact, if you are unable to answer this question, the situation would be analogous to that in which someone asserts, "It is hotter here," and yet, when questioned, holds that there need not be an implicit comparison, that to be making a significant statement he need not be *able* to make some additional statement such as "It is hotter here than there." [3]

Now it seems that the relation of resemblance belongs to this latter class of necessarily comparative relations.[4] A statement of the form *"x resembles y"* can be made intelligibly only if it is explicitly regarded as an elliptical version of a statement of the form *"x resembles y more than w resembles z"* or if the context of its use makes clear that it is such a version. At first this may seem implausible. Is it not obvious that the color of my hat resembles the color of this book? Can there be any question that we understand perfectly well what is meant by saying that the shape of one penny resembles the shape of another penny? But I believe that such rhetorical questions seem convincing only because we are already familiar with the sort of shape that a penny ordinarily has and with the sort of resemblance between

3. "X is far from *y*" could be used in the sense of "*x* is too far from *y* for such and such purposes." But this is not really a different sense. It amounts to "*x* is farther from *y* than it should be if such and such purposes are to be achieved."

4. Cf. D. J. O'Connor, "On Resemblance," *Aristotelian Society Proceedings*, 1945-46.

the color of a hat and the color of a book which, in comparison with other usual sorts of resemblances, would be noticeable. But suppose that we consider the assertion of the resemblance of two qualities a and b (e.g., two unusual tastes) with which we are not already familiar, and with regard to which we do not already have an established system of comparisons. Does the assertion mean that both are tastes or that both are sour or that both have the sourness of a pickle or that both have the sourness of a dill pickle or that both have the sourness of a particular brand of dill pickle or that the two are completely indistinguishable qualitatively? If a and b are colors, does the assertion of their resemblance mean that they are indistinguishable qualitatively or that both are a certain kind of pink or that both are pink or that both are red or that one is red and the other is orange or that both qualities happen to be colors? Clearly, the assertion could have any one of these meanings. And this means that it does not have any meaning at all.

Consider the statement "The color of my hat and the color of this book resemble each other." Clearly, a statement of this kind can occur alone and be perfectly intelligible. It need not be followed by an explicit comparison of the degree of the resemblance with some other instance of resemblance. Nor is it necessary that the speaker or the listener should be actually conscious of such a comparison. But unless such a comparison constitutes the general context of the statement, unless the two persons are talking about the resemblance of the color of the hat and the color of the book in the general context of certain instances of color-resemblance with

which both are acquainted, the statement would be essentially incomplete, it would be impossible to determine in what cases it would be true and in what cases
false. Suppose that I were to say, "The color of my hat
resembles the color of this book," and you were to ask,
"How much does it resemble it?" or, what comes to the
same thing, "It resembles it more than it resembles what
other colors?" Clearly, your question must be answered
if my statement is to be considered informative. If I
were unable to answer it, the situation would be similar to that in which someone asserts that New York is
far from Washington and yet refuses to explain, with
respect to what other city New York is far from Washington. Consider a world consisting only of the color of
my hat and the color of this book. Would the statement
that the two colors resemble each other provide us with
any information about such a world that is not already
provided by the mere listing of the two colors as its
constituents? In what circumstances would we reject this
statement as false and in what circumstances would we
accept it as true? How would we understand the difference between the statement that the two colors resemble
each other and the statement that they do not resemble
each other? It may be suggested that one could consider
other colors even if these other colors were not constituents of that world and that the resemblance of the color
of my hat and the color of this book could be asserted
in the context of the resemblances among these other
colors. But, apart from the question whether in a world
which consists only of two colors one can even consider
other colors (the sense in which a world can be said
to contain colors is obviously very different from the

sense in which a world can be said to contain John and
Mary, or color-patches), the suggestion still allows that
the assertion of the resemblance of the two colors depends for its meaningfulness on a comparison of the
degree of this resemblance with the degree of other instances of color-resemblance.[5]

Does the above constitute a return to the Nominalist
Theory? It does not. Indeed, the Nominalist Theory
regards statements of the form "x resembles y" as uninformative because of reasons which seem similar to
those I have just given. But its diagnosis is different
and so is the suggested cure. According to it, there is
no such fact as the recurrence of a quality at all, whether
it be a qualitative identity or a resemblance, unless it
is the fact of the applicability of a certain general word
to certain objects. It follows from this that a mere assertion of the resemblance of two qualities is uninformative
unless it can be taken to mean that a certain general
word or one of a certain range of general words is appli-

5. It has been suggested by C. J. Ducasse (in "Some Critical Comments
on a Nominalistic Analysis of Resemblance," *Philosophical Review*,
1940) that even if a person were aware of only two hues, he might still
be able to assert meaningfully that they resemble each other or that
they do not, by using as evidence of their resemblance his difficulty in
discriminating between them, or as evidence of their nonresemblance
the lack of such a difficulty. If he frequently mistakes one of the hues
for the other, then he would be able to consider them similar; if no
such mistakes occur, he would consider them dissimilar. I think that
Ducasse would be right if we could assume that such a person already
has the concept of similarity. Then, remembering that in other cases
close similarity is ordinarily accompanied by difficulty in discrimination,
he would infer from the presence of such a difficulty in the case of the
two hues that the two hues are similar. But it cannot be supposed that
he would be able to derive the concept of similarity from the concept
of difficulty in discrimination. And, in any case, there is a correlation
between similarity and difficulty in discrimination only if the similarity
is a rather close one.

cable to both qualities. And, according to the Nominalist Theory, a resemblance-statement, though logically incomplete in itself, can be completed only by specifying the respect of the resemblance, since such a specification amounts to indicating the general word or one of a range of general words which is applicable to the terms of the resemblance. I rejected the Nominalist Theory on the grounds that the recurrence of a quality, or the resemblance of certain qualities, is distinguishable from the fact of the applicability of a certain general word. But I agree with the Nominalist Theory that isolated statements of the form "x resembles y" are logically incomplete. Yet the kind of completion of such statements which I suggest is fundamentally different from the kind of completion suggested by the Nominalist Theory. The reason why statements of the form "x resembles y"—where x and y are simple qualities—are incomplete is that the resemblance of two qualities admits of extremely wide variation of degree, and such statements do not specify the degree of the resemblance. But to speak of the degree of an instance of resemblance is necessarily to speak of its relations to the degrees of other instances of resemblance. Therefore, to know the degree of the resemblance of a and b is to know whether the resemblance of a and b is greater or lesser than the resemblance of a and c, or of b and c, or of c and d, etc.[6] But then the degree of an instance of resemblance

6. Instead of completing "x resembles y" as "x resembles y more than w resembles z," one could in some cases complete it as "x resembles y exactly." But in reality this is not a different kind of completion. If it is not to be taken to mean that x and y are one and the same color (which would be to accept the Identity Theory), the latter statement must mean simply that x resembles y either more or as much as any w *can* resemble any z.

would not need to be specified by an indication of its respect, or of the general words applicable to both of its terms. It can be so specified in a statement of the form "x resembles y more than w resembles z," which would be logically complete and yet would be a straightforward resemblance-statement. In fact, it can be argued that this latter kind of statement is the primary kind of completion of a logically incomplete resemblance-statement of the form "x resembles y." For, what seems essential to the meaningfulness of the statement "a resembles b" is not so much the classifiability of both a and b as F, but a context in which it is clear that the statement is an elliptical version of a statement such as "a resembles b more than c." It might be argued that we can classify two colors as red only if we recognize that their resemblance is greater than, say, the resemblance of one of them and a shade of yellow.

But if resemblance is a necessarily comparative relation, i.e., if the only kind of resemblance-statement which is logically complete has the form "x resembles y more than w resembles z," the question arises whether such a peculiar relation is dyadic at all. In this respect, statements of the form "x resembles y" appear to be closely analogous to what are ordinarily called, in logic, relative terms, e.g., short, bright, large. A relative term F is such that a statement of the form "x is F" is logically incomplete and its completed form contains reference to two or more objects. To say that John is short is to say that John is shorter than someone else, e.g., Peter or the average man. And this implies that being short is not a genuine property but is an elliptical way of referring to a dyadic relation. Of course, John does have a genuine property in virtue of which he is shorter than Peter, namely the particular shape and size of his body. But *this* property is not the property of being short. Analogously, now, we must conclude that a "relative relation," a relation whose every instance must be compared in degree with another instance of the same relation, is not a genuine dyadic relation. A statement asserting the resemblance of two objects is logically incomplete, not in the Nominalist sense (which I examined in Chapter One), that the respect of the resemblance must be stated, but in the sense that such a statement is meaningful only if regarded as an elliptical version of a statement in which reference is made to at least three objects, namely, a statement of the form "x resembles y more than w resembles z," where w can be identical with x. And to have shown that statements of the form "x resembles y" are thus logically incomplete is to have shown that resemblance is not a dyadic relation. What is meant by saying that a certain relation is dyadic is that the assertion that it holds between certain two objects is logically complete, that such an assertion requires no other statement and no reference to any other object for its meaningfulness.

Is resemblance a triadic or tetradic relation, then? It has been argued that it is.[7] For while statements of the form "x resembles y" are not logically complete, statements of the form "x resembles y more than w resembles z" are logically complete; and the former can be understood only as elliptical versions of the latter. In the same way, one can argue that the relation of being-far-from

7. E.g., by D. J. O'Connor, cited.

is also a triadic or tetradic relation. For while statements of the form "x is far from y" are logically incomplete, statements of the form "x is farther from y than w is from z" are not; and the former can only be understood as elliptical versions of the latter. But all such arguments are futile. They have not the slightest tendency to show that resemblance, or remoteness, is a triadic or tetradic relation. The reason is simple. It is a logical truth that resemblance cannot *be* the relation of difference in degree between instances of resemblance, and that remoteness cannot *be* the relation of difference in degree between instances of remoteness. Yet it is precisely this that they are asserted to be by the theory which holds that resemblance and remoteness are triadic or tetradic relations. To say that a resembles b more than a resembles c is precisely to say that the resemblance between a and b is greater than the resemblance between a and c. And to say that a is farther from b than a is from c is to say that the remoteness of a from b is greater than the remoteness of a from c. Resemblance is asserted not of a, b, and c, but of a and b only, and then separately, of a and c only. The relation asserted by the statement "a is farther from b than a is from c" is intelligible only if understood as the dyadic relation of difference in degree, the terms of which are two separate instances of a dyadic relation of being-far-from, the first instance having as its terms a and b and the second instance having as its terms a and c. The relation asserted by the statement "a resembles b more than a resembles c" is also intelligible only if understood as the dyadic relation of difference in degree, the terms of which are two separate instances of a dyadic relation of resemblance, the first instance having as its terms a and b and the second instance having as its terms a and c. In a logically complete resemblance-statement the relational expression "more than" cannot refer to an aspect of the relation of resemblance; it can only refer to a second-order relation, the terms of which are two instances of a first-order relation of resemblance. Such a second-order relation can only be understood as dyadic; and the first-order relation of resemblance can only be understood as dyadic, too. But we have already seen that neither remoteness nor resemblance can be a dyadic relation.

The conclusion we seem to have reached is that resemblance is not a triadic or tetradic relation. We have also seen that it is not a dyadic relation. And there can be no likelihood that it may turn out to have more than four terms. Therefore, if it is logically necessary that a relation have a definite, clearly and unequivocally determinable number of terms, then resemblance cannot be a relation. But may we not suppose that resemblance is a unique relation, that it is quite unlike any other relation, instead of reaching the paradoxical conclusion that it is not a relation at all? A discovery of such uniqueness of the relation of resemblance would not be an ordinary discovery. For the peculiarities of resemblance because of which it would be considered unique are not the kind of peculiarities that other relations might have. They are basic, categorial peculiarities. And recognizing these peculiarities is not recognizing that resemblance is a very peculiar relation. A relation which is neither clearly dyadic, nor clearly triadic or tetradic or n-adic, is not just a peculiar relation. It is not a relation at all and statements in which reference is made to it are not relational statements. But the distinguishing character-istic of the Resemblance Theory, as we have seen, is its claim that the situations of the recurrence of qualities are very much like ordinary situations of the related-ness of distinct objects. To reach the conclusion that resemblance is not a relation is to reach the conclusion that the Resemblance Theory is false.

12. The Meaning of Resemblance-Statements

A conclusion such as the one we have reached cannot be just happily proclaimed and then seized upon as a basis of philosophical theorizing. Even if we have reached it without making mistakes about the nature of relations and the use of relational statements, its signifi-cance must be assessed carefully and with restraint. For the theory of universals it is not enough to say that necessarily comparative statements such as resemblance-statements differ from relational statements in such fun-damental respects that they should not be considered relational at all. Perhaps this would be enough for the rejection of the Resemblance Theory, since, as we have seen, it is essential to the distinctive character of the latter that resemblance be considered a relation. But it would not be enough for the purposes of presenting an adequate theory of universals. The peculiar features of resemblance-statements must be explained. If resem-blance-statements are not relational, then what does their meaning consist in? Why are there such statements at all, and not merely statements of qualitative identity?

Philosophy is the one cognitive discipline in which there is no place for mysteries. And the use of such a familiar and commonplace kind of statement as resemblance-statements can even less be a mystery. Let us begin with an explanation of the analogous case of the relation of being-far-from. Perhaps it will provide us with the clues for an adequate account of resemblance.

There is no dyadic relation of being-far-from. Nor is being-far-from a triadic or tetradic relation. And it makes no sense to suppose that it has more than four terms. Does this mean that statements of the form "*x* is far from *y*" and even statements of the form "*x* is farther from *y* than it is from *z*" are meaningless? It would be absurd to reach such a conclusion. It would also be unnecessary. For we all know quite well what is meant by a statement such as "*a* is farther from *b* than it is from *c*." Clearly, it is synonymous with the statement "The distance between *a* and *b* is greater than the distance between *a* and *c*." And in the latter the word "distance," though denoting a spatial relation which may be problematic in its own way, is not the name of the relation being-far-from. "The distance between *x* and *y*" is synonymous with "the length of the straight line connecting *x* and *y*" or "the length of the route connecting *x* and *y*" or even "the time needed for travelling between *x* and *y*." Thus it is seen that while there is not a dyadic relation such as being-far-from, nor a triadic or tetradic relation such as the one suggested by the structure of the form "*x* is farther from *y* than *w* is from *z*," statements of this form are not at all meaningless and merely constitute variants of statements of the form "The distance between x and y is greater than the distance between w and z." The latter are relational statements, the relation being that of difference in length. And statements of the form "x is farther from y than w is from z" (as well as their elliptical versions of the form "x is far from y") are also relational, but the relation they really assert is not, as one would ordinarily have supposed, the relation of being-far-from or even the relation of difference in degree between two instances of the relation of being-far-from, but, again, simply the relation of difference in length between two distances.

The above explanation of the meaning of statements of the form "x is far from y" is analogous to the explanation of the meaning of statements containing relative terms. To say that John is short is to say that he is shorter than, say, Peter. Only the latter, expanded statement is logically complete. But this does not mean that John still has a quality of being short, though it is essential that this quality be related to Peter's corresponding quality by the relation of shorter than. It is not John's shortness that is shorter than Peter's shortness. The quality of being short has been shown to be spurious and reference to it in this case has been shown to be simply a misleading way of asserting that John and Peter are related by the relation of being-shorter-than. The terms of this relation are not shortnesses. If they are not John and Peter, they are the height of John and the height of Peter.

Now, what would be the corresponding explanation of the meaning of statements of the form "x resembles y more than w resembles z"? It would seem that the key requirement which such an explanation must meet is that an expression be found whose function in the explanation of the meaning of such statements would be analogous to the function of the phrase "the distance between x and y" in the explanation of the meaning of statements of the form "x is farther from y than w is from z," or to the function of the phrase "the height of x" in the explanation of the meaning of statements of the form "x is shorter than y." Such an expression must satisfy two conditions. First, it must not refer to a relation of resemblance. (Just as "the distance between x and y" refers not to the relation of being-far-from, but, if to a relation at all, only to that of being-spatially-separated-from; and just as "the height of x" does not refer to x's property of being short.) Second, it must be such that it can occur in statements which, though not containing reference to a relation of resemblance, express faithfully the meaning of statements of the form "x resembles y more than w resembles z." (Just as "the distance between x and y" can occur in statements of the form "The distance between x and y is greater than the distance between w and z," which do not contain reference to a relation of being-far-from and yet express faithfully the meaning of statements of the form "x is farther from y than w is from z"; and just as "the height of x" can occur in statements of the form "The height of x is shorter [i.e., less] than the height of y," which do not contain reference to the shortness of x and yet express faithfully the meaning of statements of the form "x is shorter than y.") Clearly, the required expression cannot be "the resemblance between x and y." While this expression does satisfy the second condition, it fails to satisfy the first condition. Indeed, the statement "The resemblance between *a* and *b* is greater than the resemblance between *a* and *c*" would seem to express faithfully the meaning of the statement "*a* resembles *b* more than *a* resembles *c*." But it contains reference to what may only be interpreted as a relation of resemblance. Thus, instead of elucidating the meaning of the latter statement, the former statement is comprehensible only because the latter statement is comprehensible. Such an explanation of the meaning of resemblance-statements would be like explaining the meaning of "*a* is farther from *b* than it is from *c*" by translating it as "The remoteness of *a* from *b* is greater than the remoteness of *a* from *c*," or explaining the meaning of "*a* is shorter than *b*" by translating it as "*a*'s shortness is greater than *b*'s." But what other expression is there? What expression would satisfy the above two conditions? It would seem that the only other expression that could be suggested with any plausibility is "the common quality (i.e., the universal) whose instances are *x* and *y*." It satisfies the first condition. If the common quality is a specific universal, then its instances can be regarded as specifically identical. If it is a generic universal, then its instances can be regarded as generically identical. In neither case is there a possibility of confusing the identity of the instances with a relation of resemblance. For, as we have seen, what is meant by "identity," be the latter specific or only generic, is essentially incompatible with what is meant by "relation." [8] The expression "the common quality whose instances are *x* and *y*" meets also

8. See above, pp. 108-109.

the second condition. Common qualities, i.e., universals, can be compared in respect to degree of generality. A specific universal, such as a shade of pink, has the lowest possible generality; it cannot have instances which are qualitatively distinguishable. The several kinds of pink are already generic universals, though of very low generality; the instances of such a universal may have qualitative differences, though not pronounced ones. Pink has higher generality. The generality of the universal red is even higher; its instances may have considerable qualitative differences; one of them may instantiate a specific shade of pink while the other may instantiate a specific shade of crimson. Now, clearly, such levels of generality correspond to the degrees of resemblance that a logically complete resemblance-statement compares. Consequently, a statement of the form "The universal of least generality instantiated in x and in y is of lower generality than the universal of least generality instantiated in w and in z" would seem to express faithfully the meaning of a statement of the form "x resembles y more than w resembles z," assuming that both statements are about simple qualities.[9] The problem of generic universals, however, is difficult and until we examine it in detail in Chapter Four, this account of the meaning of resemblance-statements must remain incomplete.

It is tempting now to speculate about the genuine differences between the terminology of resemblances and the terminology of qualitative identities. Why are

9. The qualifying phrase "of least generality" in the above translation of a resemblance-statement is needed because, in addition to the universal of least generality instantiated in both of two qualities, all of its superordinate universals are also instantiated in these qualities. An instance of pink is also an instance of red and of color.

there two such terminologies at all? What is the explanation of the peculiarities of resemblance-statements
which we have examined? Perhaps the following possible explanation should be mentioned. In addition to
the general fact of the recurrence of qualities, there is
also the related, and equally important, fact of the differences in degree of generality among the universals
which are the recurrent qualities. The special function
of the terminology of qualitative identities would seem
to be the description of recurrences of qualities. The
special function of the terminology of resemblances
would seem to be the description of differences in degree of generality between recurrent qualities. Perhaps
this is why resemblance-statements have a necessarily
comparative character. It is perhaps also the explanation of the fact that the terminology of qualitative identities has always seemed much more suitable for the
description of cases of exact resemblance, while the terminology of resemblances has seemed more suitable for
the description of cases of inexact resemblance. The fact
that a specific universal, or a generic universal of very
low degree of generality, is instantiated in qualities of
certain two individuals can be interesting in itself and
worth describing. But the fact that a universal of relatively high degree of generality is instantiated in such
qualities would rarely be of interest. What might be of
interest, however, is the contrast between its degree of
generality and the degree of generality of some other
universal which is instantiated in one of these two
qualities and in a certain quality of a third individual.
The generic identity of the color of a pink flag and the
color of a crimson flag can hardly arouse interest if con-

sidered in isolation from other cases of generic identity, though of course it can be noticed and asserted. But it may be quite interesting when contrasted with the generic identity of the color of the pink flag and the color of a yellow flag, an identity which, presumably, consists merely in that both are colors. On the other hand, the specific identity of the color of a pair of brown trousers and the color of a brown jacket, or the generic identity of the color of a light brown jacket and a dark brown hat, may be of interest in itself and worth describing, quite apart from the relations of difference in degree of generality between the color-universal instantiated in the colors of such objects and the color-universal instantiated, e.g., in the color of the dark brown hat and in the color of a red book.

The fact that generic identity is seldom of interest in itself suggests, and also probably explains, the fact that statements of the form "x is generically identical with y" or "x and y are one and the same in general" are not less uninformative and logically incomplete than statements of the form "x resembles y" are. Any two qualities under the same *summum genus* are generically identical, and if there is only one *summum genus,* then any two qualities whatever are generically identical. Consequently, to be informative a statement which asserts the generic identity of two qualities must specify the degree of the generality of the universal which is the ground of the generic identity. Again, this degree can be specified in two ways: one can indicate the general word applicable to the instances of the universal, or one can compare the degree of generality of this universal with the degree of generality of some other universal. Again, it would seem that the latter kind of specification is the primary one. To say this, however, is not to say that the meaning of the general word can be explained non-platitudinously. It is to say only that while the latter kind of specification is logically independent of the former, the former kind of specification appears to be logically dependent on the latter. One can know that the degree of generality of the least general universal which is instantiated in the color of the pair of trousers and in the color of the jacket is lesser than the degree of generality of the least general universal which is instantiated in the color of the jacket and in the color of the hat, even if one does not know that the color of the trousers and the color of the jacket are light-brown and that the color of the hat is dark-brown. But it would seem that a necessary condition of one's knowing that the color of the trousers and the color of the jacket are light-brown and that the color of the hat is dark-brown is one's knowing that the least general universal instantiated both in the color of the trousers and in the color of the jacket is less general than the least general universal instantiated both in the color of the jacket and in the color of the hat. But while knowing the latter may be a necessary condition of knowing the former, it is not a sufficient condition. One may know that the least general universal instantiated in the color of the trousers and in the color of the jacket is less general than the least general universal instantiated in the color of the jacket and in the color of the hat and yet not know that the trousers and the jacket are light-brown and that the hat is dark-brown. And, to the extent to which this is true, the difference in degree of generality between these two universals does not provide an explanation of the meaning of the general words "light-brown" and "brown." This is the kernel of truth to be found in the Nominalist Theory.

It should be noted that the uninformative and logically incomplete character of statements of the form "x is generically identical with y" or "x and y are one and the same in general" does not imply that there is no such fact as generic identity, as the uninformative and logically incomplete character of a statement of the form "x resembles y" implies that there is no such relation as resemblance. The fact that statements of the form "x resembles y" are uninformative and logically incomplete does not imply that there is no such *fact* as resemblance, but only that resemblance is not a *relation*. It implies this because it implies that a relation of resemblance may only be a necessarily comparative relation. And, as we have seen, a necessarily comparative relation is not a relation at all, because it does not have a clearly and unequivocally determinable, definite number of terms. But *identity* is not supposed by the Identity Theory to be a relation at all, and, while one could argue that generic identity is not a relation in the same way in which I have argued that resemblance is not a relation, such an argument would only support the Identity Theory and not at all tend to show also that there is no such fact as generic identity. If there is no claim made that generic identity may only be a relation, then the logically incomplete character of statements of the form "x is generically identical with y" or "x and y are one and the same in general" would tend to prove that there is no such fact as generic identity only as

much as the logically incomplete character of statements
of the form "x resembles y" tends to prove that there
is no such *fact* as resemblance. As we saw in the beginning of this chapter, to deny that there is a relation of
resemblance is not to deny that there is such a fact as
resemblance—it is only to deny that this fact is classifiable as a relation. But no attempt to assert that identity
is a relation is either made here or ought to be made.
On the other hand, denying that there is such a fact as
generic identity or that there is such a fact as resemblance, on the ground that merely asserting that two
qualities are generically identical or that they resemble
each other tells us nothing about the qualities, would be
like denying that there is such a fact as degree of temperature or height of a person, on the ground that to
say merely that an object has degree of temperature or
that a person has height tells us nothing about the object or the person. If degrees of temperature or heights
of persons can be compared, then there are degrees of
temperature and heights of persons. If resemblances or
generic identities can be compared, then there are resemblances and generic identities.

13. Generic, Abstract, and Intelligible
Universals

Our conclusion that resemblance is not a relation has provided us with what appears to be an excellent reason for rejecting the Resemblance Theory. For, as we have seen, the Resemblance Theory has an intelligible and distinctive character only in so far as it claims that resemblance is a relation. We have also found fatal defects in the Nominalist Theory. Does it follow, then, that we ought to accept the Identity Theory? There would seem to be no further reason for questioning the account of exact resemblance which the Identity Theory offers. But its account of inexact resemblance has special difficulties of considerable gravity. There is one major objection to the possibility of generic identity which does not exist with respect to the possibility of specific identity; the existence of generic universals appears questionable in one respect in which the existence of specific universals does not appear questionable. While the sense in which specific universals can be said to be observable is quite similar to that in which other objects are said to be observable, the sense in which generic universals can be said to be observable is very different, so different indeed that one may be unwilling to call generic universals observable at all.

Although empiricism has often been associated with the rejection of the Identity Theory, it should be obvious that the Identity Theory is perfectly compatible with empiricism in so far as it asserts that there are specific universals. A specific shade of color is an object of direct sensory awareness even if it is instantiated in several locally separate individuals. It seems quite unjustified to argue that one cannot observe universals because one cannot observe anything which is separate from individuals. It is the qualities of individuals that the Identity Theory claims to be universals. And while, in this sense, it is true that no universal can be observed as separate from an individual, it is also true that no individual can be observed as separate from universals. It is equally unjustified to argue that, since one can observe a universal only in so far as it is instantiated in an individual, and since a universal can be instantiated in an indefinite number of individuals, therefore one can never observe the whole or complete being of a universal, i.e., the universal as such, by merely observing an instance of it.[1] Such an argument is based on a misunderstanding. To say that there are universals, that the qualities of individuals are universals, that a universal can be instantiated at many places at the same time, is precisely to say that certain qualities of certain

1. Cf. E. D. Klemke, "Universals and Particulars in a Phenomenalist Ontology," *Philosophy of Science*, 1960.

individuals are identical, that it is possible for a quality of one individual to be identical with a quality of another individual, that the instances of a recurrent quality are identical. But if this is so, then it would be nonsense to claim that in observing an instance of a universal one is not observing the whole and complete being of the universal. If there is a sense in which certain qualities of distinct individuals are identical, then there is a corresponding sense in which observing one of them is identical with observing all of them, i.e., with observing the universal whose instances they constitute. Thus, the problem of specific universals is independent of the problem of the acceptability of empiricism. One can accept the existence of specific universals and still be an empiricist. But the case with generic universals appears to be very different. There are good reasons for thinking that even if the instances of a generic universal are observable, the generic universal itself is not. There are good reasons for thinking that one cannot observe color which is neither red, nor blue, nor white, nor any other determinate color, that one cannot observe triangularity which is neither equilateral, nor equicrural, nor scalene. It is because there are good reasons for denying that generic universals are observable that empiricism has been closely associated with the rejection of the Identity Theory.

What reasons have prompted philosophers to consider generic universals unobservable? I think that the main reason can be explained as follows. Consider two specifically different qualities, the pink color of one object and the crimson color of another object, which may be said to be one and the same general color because both

are red. *Ex hypothesi,* the two colors are different not
only in the sense in which one may wish to say that the
color of region 1 and the color of region 4 are different
but *also* in the sense in which one would say that the
color of region 1 and the color of region 3 are different.[2]
The Identity Theory asserts that local separation is not
a sufficient reason for regarding the color of region 1
and the color of region 4 as two distinct colors. And
since, presumably, no other reason can be given for
denying the identity of the color of region 1 and the
color of region 4, it concludes that the two colors are
one and the same color. Now, if the color of 1 and
the color of 4 need not be considered different merely
because they are locally separate, then surely it follows
also that the color of 1 and the color of 3 need not be
considered different merely because they are locally separate. But in the latter case there is one other reason for
considering the two colors different, a reason which does
not exist in the former case. The color of 1 and the color
of 3 are not only locally separate but also qualitatively
different. Nevertheless, the Identity Theory asserts that
there is a sense in which the color of 1 and the color of
3 are one and the same color (i.e., red). And to say this
it must claim not only that local separation is not a
sufficient condition of qualitative nonidentity, but also
that even a certain kind of qualitative difference is not
a sufficient condition of nonidentity. And the special difficulties of the Identity Theory with regard to generic
universals begin here. Qualitative difference is not at all
analogous to local separation, and cannot be explained
away in the manner in which the latter can. One can

2. See above, pp. 58-65.

meaningfully claim that two color-patches (e.g., regions 1 and 4) are different only *qua* surface regions and that their colors themselves are not different; one can make this claim because one can distinguish without difficulty between the color and the spatial characteristics of a color-patch—one can vary the size or shape of a color-patch without varying its color and one can vary its color without varying its size and shape. The defender of specific universals can relegate the difference between the qualities whose identity he defends to something which is obviously distinguishable from the qualities, namely, to the spatial regions occupied by them. But the defender of generic universals cannot resolve his difficulties in this way. The differences which he must explain away can be relegated neither to the spatial regions occupied by the qualities whose generic identity he defends, nor to anything else that is distinguishable from the qualities themselves, for they are differences *within* the qualities.

How can the Identity Theory still defend its claim that two specifically different qualities may be identical? The defense which it proposes is well known. According to it, generic identity is not simple and immediate as specific identity is. Generically identical qualities do not instantiate only the universal which is the ground of their identity. They also instantiate certain specific universals, which are the ground of their diversity. The pink color of one object and the crimson color of another object are not merely instances of red. The former is also an instance of a certain specific shade of pink and the latter is an instance of a certain specific shade of crimson. The two colors are qualitatively different because the one is an instance of a shade of pink and the other is an instance of a shade of crimson. But they are identical because both are also instances of red. Thus, to explain the possibility of the generic identity of two qualities such as the pink color of one object and the crimson color of another object, the Identity Theorist asserts that each quality is an instance of at least two universals, the instantiation of one of which is the ground of the quality's diversity from the other quality, while the instantiation of the other universal is the ground of the quality's identity with the other quality. In this way he rests the adequacy of his account of in-exact resemblance on the truth of the assertion that in the pink color of one object and the crimson color of another object there are instantiated at least three uni-versals: a specific shade of pink, a specific shade of crimson, and the generic quality red. But can one claim that in observing the pink object and the crimson object one is observing three color-qualities, three color-uni-versals? To most philosophers it has seemed obvious that in such a situation one observes only the specific shade of pink and the specific shade of crimson. And for this reason they have thought that by proposing the above account of inexact resemblance the defender of generic universals has been forced to say that the generic identity of two observable qualities of individual things is itself unobservable. Some philosophers have taken this consequence to mean that there are not cases of generic identity, that there are not generic universals. Other philosophers have taken it to mean that the ground of the order and the knowability of the observable world is itself unobservable.

To avoid the above consequence, the Identity Theorist has sometimes claimed that the generic universal red, because of which a pink shade and a crimson shade can be said to be one and the same general color, is an observable distinct component of the specific shades of red. Each shade of red consists of at least two components, one of which is peculiar to it and constitutes its specific characteristic, and the other of which is its generic characteristic, that which it shares with all other shades of red. The redness of a shade of pink and a shade of crimson, according to this theory, is not external to the two shades, and this is why in observing instances of the latter we observe only two qualities and not three. At the same time, however, it is an observable distinct element *within* each shade, and our perception of the identity of this element in the shade of pink and in the shade of crimson constitutes our reason for regarding both shades as red. Thus the basic claim of this peculiar version of the Identity Theory, which may be called the Theory of Abstract Universals, is that generic identity is reducible to partial specific identity. The pink color of one object is generically identical with the crimson color of another object in the sense that a certain observable distinct component of the specific shade which is instantiated in the one is specifically identical with a certain observable distinct component of the specific shade which is instantiated in the other. The difference between this kind of specific identity and the specific identity which we have considered hitherto is that in the latter a quality of an individual is specifically identical with a quality of another individual, while in the former a component (doubtless, itself qualitative) of a quality is specifically identical with a component of another quality.

Sometimes the Theory of Abstract Universals is brushed aside as obviously false because it is assumed that qualities do not have the sort of observable complexity which according to the theory they must have. But it is not obvious that this assumption is true. For instance, specific shades of color are ordinarily understood as determined by the factors of hue, saturation, and brilliance; that these factors are observably distinguishable is shown by the fact that one of them can be varied, within certain limits, independently of the other two, and by the possibility of fairly detailed classificatory systems of color such as the Munsell system.[3] Indeed, their diversity is not a spatial one, they do not occupy different spaces; but there are many familiar cases of perfectly genuine nonspatial kinds of observable diversity, e.g., the sourness and sweetness of lemonade. Sounds have pitch, loudness and timbre. Tastes and smells can be classified in terms of specific nature, intensity, and purity. And there is no clear reason why such easily distinguishable observable characteristics of sense-qualities should not be considered to be their distinct components, each sense-quality being a kind of mixture of several simpler observable qualities. Thus, a specific shade of color can be regarded as a "mixture" of a certain hue, a certain degree of saturation, and a certain degree of brilliance; and a specific kind of sound can be regarded as a mixture of a certain pitch, a certain timbre, and a certain degree of loudness.

3. Cf. the color plates in *The Munsell Book of Color* (Baltimore: Munsell Color Company, 1929).

But even if it is admitted that the specific qualities with which we are familiar are qualitative mixtures of observable distinct components, the Theory of Abstract Universals would still be faced with difficulties. For the components of complex qualities may themselves enter in relations of inexact resemblance. And how then would the theory account for such instances of inexact resemblance? Two qualitatively distinguishable colors may resemble each other inexactly not only because the hue of the one is specifically identical with the hue of the other, but also because the hue of the one resembles *inexactly* the hue of the other. And even if we can regard the hue of a color as an observable distinct component of it, surely we cannot claim that there is also an *observable* complexity in the hues themselves, that two inexactly resembling hues contain an observable distinct component which is specifically identical in both. Two colors may also resemble each other because the brilliance of the one resembles inexactly the brilliance of the other; and surely we cannot find a distinguishable component of the brilliance of the one color which is specifically identical with a distinguishable component of the brilliance of the other color. Two sounds may resemble each other inexactly because they have a specifically identical pitch, but they may also resemble each other because the pitch of the one resembles inexactly the pitch of the other; and it would seem absurd to look for a complexity in the pitch of a sound, which would be such that an observable distinct component of the pitch of the one sound would be specifically identical with an observable distinct component of the pitch of the other sound.

Therefore, to defend its adequacy, the Theory of Abstract Universals must assert either that there are no cases of inexact resemblance between qualities in which no complexity is observable, or that abstract universals may be unobservable, intelligible entities. The first assertion obviously flies in the face of empirical fact and requires no further discussion. The second assertion, however, is subtler. It amounts to a courageous acceptance of what most philosophers have considered to be the unavoidable consequence of an Identity Theory of inexact resemblance. The thesis of the theory now is that even the inexact resemblance of qualities which have no observable complexity can be explained as the presence in them of an abstract universal. The inexact resemblance of the hue of one shade of color and the hue of another shade cannot consist in the specific identity of an observable distinct component of the one hue and an observable distinct component of the other hue, because no distinct components in the hues are observable. But why should such a component be observable at all? It can be an unobservable entity known only through the intellect. And then the fact that we do not observe it as a distinct element in its instances would not be an objection to the theory.

Thus we are faced with another version of the Identity Theory of inexact resemblance, which may be called the Theory of Intelligible Universals. Its history is long and distinguished, and there is nothing fanciful about it. There are cases of inexact resemblance. Most of them cannot be accounted for in terms of the specific identity of some observable distinct components of the resembling qualities. At the same time, because of the conclusions we reached in Chapter Three, such cases cannot be regarded as the relatedness of distinct qualities by a special relation of resemblance. Then what other alternative is there? It seems only natural to suppose that such cases of resemblance are to be explained as the presence in the resembling qualities of an unobservable universal. If all resemblance may only be qualitative identity, and if we cannot observe the identity of some resembling qualities, then their identity may only be unobservable.

It is sometimes thought that the general acceptability of empiricism as an epistemological doctrine is the only relevant consideration in the discussion of the possibility of unobservable universals. If one is an empiricist, either one has to reject the possibility of generic identity or one has to show that generic identities are observable. If one is not an empiricist, one can accept the possibility of generic identity with a clear conscience. But this is confused thinking. First of all, the acceptability of empiricism is largely dependent on the latter's ability to account for our knowledge of such facts as generic identities or inexact resemblances. Secondly, and more importantly, even if empiricism is rejected, one still cannot accept the existence of unobservable generic identity with a clear conscience. The characteristic of being observable is not a relatively minor characteristic which may be present in some members of a class and not in others. It is not merely a fact that no cats are unobservable. An unobservable cat is not a cat which has a certain peculiar characteristic, unobservability; it is not a cat at all. The difficulty of accepting the possibility of unobservable generic identity is neither the implied rejection of empiricism nor the difficulty of conceiving of such a peculiar kind of identity; it is the difficulty of making sense of the suggestion that *observable* qualities can be identical *unobservably*. We have approached the problem of universals by asking for the correct description of the recurrence of qualities. Consider the case of specific identity. We discover what the color of region 1 and the color of region 4 are by *observation*. And, it would be absurd to say that while the two colors are observable, their identity, i.e., the color common to both region 1 and region 4, is unobservable. But the case of generic identity is not different in this respect. It is just as absurd to say that the generic identity of the color of region 1 and the color of region 3, i.e., the general color common to the two regions, is unobservable. For, again, we discover what the color of region 1 and the color of region 3 are by observation. And only by observation can we discover the relationship of recurrence between them. Therefore, the particular description of that relationship which we may give must also be based on observation. In general, it is nonsensical to say that the instances of a recurrent quality may be observable but that their relationship of recurrence need not be. But what is meant by generic identity is precisely the recurrence of qualities such as the color of region 1 and the color of region 3. Therefore, it is also nonsensical to say that if two qualities, which are generically identical, are observable, their identity or the common quality instantiated in both need not be also observable. Perhaps there are unobservable universals. But then the instances of such universals must also be unobservable. Once this is understood, and once it is also understood that the only possible reason we have for supposing that there are universals at all is the fact of the recurrences of qualities, the temptation to look for unobservable universals behind the recurrences of the observable qualities of observable individual things would disappear.

Therefore, the question whether there is a clear sense in which the generic identity of qualities can be said to be observable is a crucial question. If there is no such sense, if there is no sense in which generic universals can be called observable, then the account of inexact resemblance which is offered by the Identity Theory must be rejected.[4]

14. The Genus-Species Relationship

The inexact resemblance of a quality of one individual and a quality of another individual cannot be intelligibly classified as a relation; for such a relation would not have a clearly and unequivocally determinable, definite number of terms. Therefore, it may only be classified as a kind of identity. And, as we have seen, to classify the inexact resemblance of two qualities as identity is to assert that, in addition to the specific universals whose instances the qualities are, there is instantiated in both qualities also a third universal, which is the ground of their identity. What is the relationship between the specific universals and the generic uni-

4. But is not this conclusion relevant only to the generic identity of *observable* qualities of individual things? Yes, indeed. We must remember, however, that, for example, in addition to the color of a pen, its shape and its being a pen are also observable. And so is my pens' being three-in-number.

versal? This is the central problem of the Identity Theory with respect to generic identity. We have already rejected two possible solutions of it. It cannot be that the generic universal and the appropriate specific universal are observable distinct components of each quality; for there are inexactly resembling qualities in which no such complexity is observed. Nor can it be that the generic universal, which constitutes the ground of the identity of the two qualities, is unobservable, while the qualities themselves and the specific universals are observable; for it is unintelligible to suppose that the recurrence or identity of observable qualities may itself be unobservable. Consequently, an adequate theory of generic identity must claim that both the generic universal and the specific universals which are instantiated in two inexactly resembling qualities are observable and yet that there need not be an observable complexity in the qualities. It seems clear that such a claim would be intelligible only if the generic universal is in some sense identical with each one of the two specific universals. Yet the identity of the generic universal with the specific universals must not be literal, complete identity, for then the specific universals themselves would be literally and completely identical and the two inexactly resembling qualities would resemble each other exactly. Thus if m and n are the specific universals which are respectively instantiated in two inexactly resembling qualities, and F is the generic universal in virtue of which the two qualities are resembling, an adequate theory of generic identity must defend the following three propositions about the relationship between F, on one hand, and m and n, on the other: (1) if m and n are observable, then F is also observable; (2) in some sense F is identical with m and with n; and (3) in some sense F is different from m and from n. Proposition (1) is really the crucial one. Were it unnecessary, any case of inexact resemblance could be explained quickly as the presence in the inexactly resembling qualities of some unobservable universal, which is different from the specific universals that constitute the ground of the diversity of the qualities and yet is present together with them in the qualities. Proposition (2) specifies what appears to be the only possible defense of proposition (1), short of subscribing to the obviously false view that there is an observable difference between the generic universal and the specific universals in all cases of inexactly resembling qualities. For if there is a sense in which the generic universal can be said to be identical with the specific universals, then, assuming that the specific universals are themselves observable, there would be a corresponding sense in which the generic universal can be said to be observable. Proposition (3), however, provides a necessary qualification of proposition (2) by demanding that the generic universal be also different from the specific universals, that it be identical with them only *in a sense* and not literally. For, the specific universals are different from one another; the resemblance which is to be accounted for is only inexact resemblance; and the identity to which the resemblance is reducible is only generic, and not specific, identity. But how can proposition (3) be reconciled with proposition (2)? This is the major difficulty of the Identity

Theory with respect to generic identity. To be observable, the generic universal in two inexactly resembling qualities must be identical with the specific universals which are necessarily also instantiated in the qualities. But if it is a generic universal at all, it must also be different from them. How can it be both? This is, in fact, the traditional problem of the nature of the genus-species relation. How can a genus be both identical with its species and yet different from them? The history of the attempt to explain how this is possible is illustrious.

Aristotle: "Evidently, therefore, with reference to that which is called the genus, none of the species-of-a-genus is either the same as it or other than it in species (and this is fitting; for the matter is indicated by negation, and the genus is the matter of that of which it is called the genus, not in the sense in which we speak of the genus or family of the Heraclidae, but in that in which the genus is an element in a thing's nature), nor is it so with reference to things which are not in the same genus, but it will differ in *genus* from them, and in species from things in the same genus." [5] Thomas Aquinas: ". . . the unity of the genus proceeds from its very indetermination and indifference; not, however, because that which is signified by genus is one nature by number in different species to which supervenes something else which is the difference determining it, as for instance form determines matter which is numerically one; but because genus signifies some form, though not determinately this or that (form) which difference expresses

5. *Met.* 1058a 21-26, trans. W. D. Ross, in *The Works of Aristotle,* Vol. 8 (Oxford: The Clarendon Press, 1928).

determinately, which is none other than that (form) which is signified indeterminately through genus." [6] Hegel: ". . . the genus is unchanged in its species; and the species are not different from the universal, but only one from another." [7] John Cook Wilson: "The genus includes all there is in the species, there is nothing left over. The differentia cannot be separated from the genus as something added on to it, it comes from within it. The species is a necessary development of the genus; even and odd are not outside number but necessitated by its nature as number, line as line must be straight or curved, it does not wait to receive this determination from something outside itself." [8] H. W. B. Joseph: "The 'class' to which species (or individuals) are referred is apt not to be thought of as something realized in its various members in a particular way; but the genus is something realized in every species (or, if it is preferred, in the individuals of every species) belonging to them, only realized in each in a special way. The differentia carries out as it were and completes the genus. . . . To define anything then *per genus et differentiam* is to put forward first a relatively vague notion and as it were the rough plan of the thing, and then to render this definite by stating in what way the rough plan is realized or worked out. And the differentiae are of the essence of the things, because they belong to the working out of this rough plan." [9] Brand Blanshard: "The universal is

6. *Concerning Being and Essence,* trans. George G. Leckie (New York: Appleton-Century-Crofts, Inc., 1937), p. 13.

7. *Science of Logic,* Vol. II, trans. W. H. Johnston and L. G. Struthers (New York: The Macmillan Company, 1929), p. 240.

8. *Statement and Inference,* p. 359.

9. *An Introduction to Logic,* pp. 85-86.

thus *in* its differentiations; it is *identical* with them; it is *distinct* from them. Call that paradox if you will; but take it with its commentary and the paradox is merely verbal." [10]

There is little doubt that the account of the genus-species relation which is suggested by the above theories is the required one.[11] At the same time, this account must be made explicit and brought into clearer connection with the fact of the recurrence of qualities, which is our only reason for supposing that there is a genus-species relationship at all, that there are generic universals and specific universals. It is not sufficiently illuminating to say that the species are a "realization" or "differentiation" or "development" of the genus, or that the genus-species relationship is a kind of "matter-form" or "plan-fulfillment" or "determinable-determinate" relation. And it must not be supposed that the sense in which the genus may be said to be both identical with and different from its species can be understood in abstraction from the sense in which certain qualities

10. *The Nature of Thought*, Vol. I, p. 611.

11. Some philosophers (e.g., John Searle, "On Determinables and the Notion of Resemblance," *Proceedings of the Aristotelian Society*, 1959) distinguish sharply between the genus-species relation and the determinable-determinate relation, on the ground that the differentia is logically independent of the genus, while there is nothing in the determinate which is logically independent of the appropriate determinable. I think that this distinction ignores the traditional account of the genus-species relation as the latter has been illustrated by the above quotations. But the distinction is made plausible, perhaps, by the natural supposition that species and genera are "substantive universals," while determinables and determinates are "qualitative universals;" and by a conception of the substantive universal as a collection of qualitative universals, which if true would render the generic identity of substantive universals explainable in terms of the Theory of Abstract Universals.

of individual things can be said to be both qualitatively identical and qualitatively different.

15. The Conditions of Generic Identity

The sense in which two specifically different qualities may be said to be identical must not be very unlike the sense in which individuals may be said to be identical. For it is the identity of individuals that constitutes the paradigm of identity. To demonstrate that certain specifically different qualities may be said to be identical is to demonstrate that such qualities are in certain essential respects like an-individual-as-it-exists-at-one-time and the-individual-as-it-exists-at-another-time or like an-individual-as-it-is-viewed-from-one-point-of-view and the-individual-as-it-is-viewed-from-another-point-of-view. At the same time, it is clear that the sense in which two specifically different qualities can be said to be identical must also be different in some important respects both from the sense in which individuals can be said to be identical and from the sense in which qualities such as the color of region 1 and the color of region 4 can be said to be identical. Otherwise the identity of the specifically different qualities would be specific and not generic identity, and thus they would not be specifically different.

It is generally assumed that the necessary condition of the identity of any entities a and b is that all characteristics of a are also characteristics of b and all characteristics of b are also characteristics of a. Perhaps in the case of the identity of individuals this condition is not also a sufficient condition, because of (1) the peculiar status of the spatial and temporal positions of the individual, and (2) the puzzling nature of the "togetherness" of the characteristics of the individual. In the case of the identity of qualities, however, there seems to be no reason for supposing that the above necessary condition of identity is not also a sufficient condition. If the color of region 1 and the color of region 4 are indeed indistinguishable, i.e., if all the characteristics of the one are characteristics of the other and *vice versa,* as the Identity Theory sometimes holds, this would constitute perfectly sufficient reason for regarding them as identical. As we have seen, it is not the adequacy of this criterion that the Resemblance Theory has questioned, but the correctness of the assumption that two locally separate qualities can be indistinguishable; for one may claim that they *are* distinguishable in terms of their different spatial locations. Now, if we adopt this criterion of identity, is there a sense in which any specifically different qualities can be called identical? It would seem that there is not. For to say that such qualities are specifically different is precisely to say that one of them has at least one characteristic which the other one does not have. But this version of the criterion of identity is oversimplified.

To say that *a* and *b* can be regarded as identical only if nothing can be said about the one that cannot be said about the other is to make the term "identical" totally inapplicable. The very possibility of the use of the word "identical" implies that a distinction is made between the objects which are said to be identical. To say that the man I am talking to now is the same as the man I saw yesterday implies the distinction between the-man-I-am-talking-to-now and the-man-I-saw-yesterday.

To say that this is the same color as that is to distinguish between this color and that. Without a distinction between *a* and *b*, one could neither think nor say that *a* and *b* are identical. It would be a serious mistake to suppose that this is a distinction not between objects or things which are said to be identical, but between "presentations" or "views" or "manners of being referred to" of one and the same object. When I assert the identity of the man I saw yesterday and the man I am talking to now, I am asserting the identity of a man, not that of his presentations or views or manners of being referred to. In fact, it would be simply false to assert the identity of the latter. In a true assertion of the identity of *a* and *b*, the symbols *a* and *b* must be different ways of referring to the same object; but they refer to the object itself, not to ways of referring to the object, or to literally different views or presentations of the object. There are two extreme philosophical theories based on these peculiarities of identity-statements. According to one, every assertion of identity is self-contradictory, and this implies that one should never think or say that something is identical with something else. According to the other, identity implies difference, but also difference implies identity, and that far from being self-contradictory, this fact is of the very essence of thought and discourse. Neither of these theories is relevant to our topic. Our purpose is much more limited. We are not concerned with the general question of the nature of statements of identity. We are concerned with the question of the similarity between cases in which, e.g., two different shades of red might be said to be identical and cases in which the-man-I-am-talking-to-now and the-

man-I-saw-yesterday would be said to be identical. If
there is something wrong with statements about identity
in general, no doubt there would be something wrong
also with statements about generic identity. But if cases
of generic identity are sufficiently like cases of individual
identity, then whatever the resolution of the difficulties
with the latter, such would also be the resolution of the
difficulties with the former. The Identity Theory would
be upheld if it is shown that situations of inexact resemblance are sufficiently like situations ordinarily described as situations of identity; this alone is of importance to the theory of universals, and the Identity
Theory would be untouched by a theory which for some
reason denies that even the latter situations are cases of
identity.

But, while any assertion of the identity of two objects
implies also a distinction between the two objects, this
distinction is quite different from that between two objects which would not ordinarily be said to be identical.
In what does this difference consist? It consists in the
supposition that the distinction between two identical
objects is only in respect to characteristics that are accidental to their being the objects they are. The difference between the man I saw yesterday and the same man
to whom I am talking now rests on the different spatiotemporal locations of the two, or on the different ways
in which they are dressed, etc.; and such characteristics
are considered accidental to a person, in the sense that
they may change or be replaced by other characteristics
and the person would still remain the same person. The
difference between the color of region 1 and the color of
region 4 rests on the different spatial locations of the

two colors; and, if the Identity Theory is right, differences in spatial location between qualities are accidental to the being of the qualities what they are. The problem of the criteria determining the distinction between the essential and accidental characteristics of an object is difficult. In one acute form it is the problem of the individuality of individuals. In another, it is the problem of specific universals. Clearly, the question whether inexact resemblance is generic identity is not independent of the general question of the criteria for the distinction between essential and accidental characteristics: if one claims that two specifically different qualities are generically identical, one must show that the characteristics in terms of which the qualities differ are in some sense accidental to their being the qualities they are. And, it may be asked, if we are not clear about the criteria of this distinction with respect to the paradigm of identity, namely, the identity of individuals, can we be clear about the criteria of this distinction with regard to generic identity? Fortunately, the difficulty is not at all as serious as it appears to be. First, the vagueness of the distinction between the essential and accidental characteristics of an individual thing is due to the enormous complexity of its nature and to the unique role of its spatiotemporal location, neither of which would be found in qualities. And, secondly, what is puzzling is not the distinction itself in general, but its application to specific subject matters. And there is no reason to suppose that its application to qualities would be as difficult as its application to individuals is.

If an ascription of identity to two specifically different qualities is to be at all justifiable, there must be a distinction between the essential and accidental characteristics of each quality. The former must be shared by both qualities: otherwise there would be no sense in the application of the word "identity" to them. But, also, the characteristics with respect to which the qualities differ must not be supposed to be entirely accidental to the latter's being the qualities they are, for then the identity of the qualities would be supposed to be specific and not generic. Clearly, the distinction between essential and accidental characteristics on the basis of which two qualities can be said to be generically identical may only be *analogous* to this distinction with respect to individuals, sufficiently like the latter in order to permit our classification of inexact resemblance as identity, and yet sufficiently unlike it in order that inexact resemblance may be classified as generic, and not specific, identity. Is there such a distinction?

We are concerned with the possibility of the generic identity of simple qualities. As we saw in Chapter One, the recurrence of simple qualities is the fundamental kind of recurrence. Other situations which are sometimes described with the terminology of resemblance, or the terminology of qualitative identities, are reducible to such recurrences. Two individuals may be said to resemble each other only in so far as certain qualities of the one individual resemble or are identical with certain qualities of the other individual. Complex qualities can be regarded as combinations or mixtures of simple qualities, and the recurrence of the former must be reducible to the recurrence of the latter. But in what sense can a simple quality have characteristics? It might seem that if a quality is simple then it can have only one char-

acteristic, namely, the characteristic of being the quality
it is. If so, it would be impossible to distinguish between
essential and accidental characteristics of a simple quality and, therefore, two qualitatively different simple
qualities could not be said to be identical in the sense
that they have their essential characteristics in common
and differ only in respect to their accidental characteristics. Of course, a multiplicity of characteristics can be
found even in a simple quality if we take into consideration its external relations to other objects, e.g., the
characteristics of two shades of red of being liked by
Mary. But we have seen that there is a clear distinction
between the internal and external resemblance of qualities.[12] And the only kind of generic identity in which
the theory of universals is interested is the generic identity of qualities in their intrinsic nature. But precisely
in its intrinsic nature a simple quality seems either to
have no characteristics or to have only one characteristic
—the characteristic of being what it is.

Nevertheless, even a simple quality can be described
with the application of several predicates. A specific
shade of color may be described as crimson, but also as
red, as color, and even as quality. At the same time it is
clear that the applicability of several such predicates to
one and the same quality does not at all render the latter
complex. For, in a fairly clear sense, all of these predicates apply to the quality itself as a whole—they all apply to the same thing. Yet they are not synonymous;
there are qualities which are not colors, colors which
are not red, and red colors which are not crimson. But,
then, the applicability of several non-synonymous predi-

12. See pp. 42-43.

cates to a simple quality would seem to imply that after all a simple quality does have several characteristics in its intrinsic nature. How would this be possible? We have already answered this question. As we saw in Chapter One,[13] the characteristics which belong to a simple quality in virtue of its intrinsic nature constitute a series the members of which differ only in respect to their generality and are not logically independent of one another. This is why the possession of several such characteristics is not incompatible with the simplicity of the quality. Being pink and being red are not two logically independent characteristics and do not constitute a complexity in the quality which is pink and red. For to be pink is to be red, and to be red is necessarily to be also either pink or some other color of the determinate range of red colors. *What* is pink and *what* is red in the quality are totally indistinguishable. Now the characteristic of lowest generality in such a series is in fact the quality itself: for a quality is not to its characteristics as an individual is to its qualities. Let us call this characteristic the specific characteristic of the quality; clearly, a quality can have only one specific characteristic. Its other characteristics would be ordered in accordance with their generality, e.g., crimson, red, color. They may be called generic characteristics. Now, the characteristics which two specifically different qualities can have in common may only be generic characteristics. And, again, the characteristics with regard to which such two specifically different qualities would differ would be their specific characteristics and perhaps some generic characteristics of lower generality than their common charac-

13. See pp. 43-45.

teristics. The generic characteristics would be generic universals, and the specific characteristics would be specific universals. And the fact that the generic characteristics and the specific characteristic of a quality are not logically independent of one another indicates that the distinction between them is not at all a covert acceptance of the Theory of Abstract Universals, but represents a version of the traditional theory of the genus-species relationship.[14]

Now, the first condition of describing two specifically different qualities as identical would be that they must have at least one generic characteristic in common; if they do not meet this condition, there would be no possibility of plausibly extending the sense of "identity," as this word is used with regard to individuals and the instances of specific universals, to apply to the relationship of two specifically different qualities. The second condition is that the two qualities must not have common specific characteristics; otherwise they would not be specifically different. The third condition, which is also the crucial one, is that the noncommon, specific characteristics of the two qualities be in some sense logically dependent on, or secondary to, their common generic characteristic, and yet be essential to the quality's being what it is. The reasons for this third condition are several. First, if the specific characteristic of the quality is logically distinct from its generic characteristic, then, as we have seen, the quality cannot be a simple

14. Of course, the above distinction between specific and generic characteristics cannot be used in a proof that there are generic universals. But here I am not pursuing such a proof, but merely the elucidation of the relation between specific and generic universals, the proof of the *intelligibility* of this relation.

one, for it would have at least two components: the generic characteristic and the specific characteristic. Second, if the specific characteristic is not in some sense logically dependent on, or secondary to, the generic characteristic, the distinction between the two would not be at all analogous to the distinction between the accidental and the essential characteristics of an individual. Third, if the specific characteristic of one quality is not at the same time essential to the quality's being what it is, then the identity of the two qualities would be specific and not generic. But what exactly would such a peculiar logical relationship between the generic and specific characteristics of a quality be? The required relation between a generic characteristic G of a simple quality and a specific characteristic H of the same simple quality can be defined as follows: (1) if a quality has H then it also has G, (2) if a quality has G then it also has one, and only one, specific characteristic ϕ such that if a quality has ϕ then it also has G.

Does the relationship between the common, generic and noncommon, specific characteristics of inexactly resembling qualities meet the above two conditions? It seems that it does. Consider the color of region 1 and the color of region 3. Both colors are red. But they differ because they are different shades of red. Both characteristics, being-red and being-the-shade-it-is, are essential to the color's being what it is. If the color of region 1 were not red, it would not be this specific color of region 1 at all. But neither would it be this specific color of region 1 if it were not the shade of red which it is. Now to the extent to which the specific characteristic of the color of region 1, which it does not have in common with the color of region 3, is essential to it, the two colors cannot be said to be identical. But there is a sense in which such noncommon, specific characteristics may be regarded as dependent on, or secondary to, their common generic characteristics, and thus there is a sense, although peculiar, in which such noncommon characteristics can be said to be accidental. The color of region 1 is the specific shade it is only because it is a shade of red. The characteristic of being this specific shade of red can be understood only by reference to the characteristic of being red; the former is not really different from the latter, but constitutes a natural specification of the latter. Being a certain shade of red entails being red. On the other hand, the characteristic of being red need not be understood by reference to the characteristic of being the specific shade of red which the color of region 1 is, it does not have to be specified in any of its instances in this particular way and not in any other. Being red does not entail being *this* shade of red. To the extent to which this is the case, the specific characteristic of the color of region 1 because of which it differs from the color of region 3 can be regarded as "accidental" to it, and thus the color of region 1 can be regarded as identical with the color of region 3. In this respect, the distinction between the generic and specific characteristics of a simple quality is seen to be *analogous* to, though of course still very different from, the distinction between the characteristics of an individual thing which are essential to its being the individual thing it is and the characteristics which are accidental to its being the individual thing it is. Two generically identical qualities have in common those characteristics which, so to speak, constitute the basis of the characteristics in respect to which they differ. Their differences appear to be derivative from their samenesses, to be logically dependent upon the latter. In a sense, the whole nature of each quality consists in its generic characteristics, in the characteristics which it may have in common with the other quality; its noncommon characteristics are not outside its common characteristics but within them. In their "essence" two such qualities are identical, and they differ only in respect to their "accidents."

At the same time, however, the noncommon, specific characteristics of two generically identical qualities are still such that the qualities would not be what they are without them. And this fact is indicated by the second aspect of the logical relationship between the generic and the specific characteristics of a simple quality. Indeed, the possession of the generic characteristic is entailed by the possession of the specific characteristic; the latter is dependent on the former. But while the possession of the generic characteristic does not entail the possession of any particular specific characteristic, and to that extent it is logically independent of the possession of any particular specific characteristic, it does entail the possession of some one and only one of a certain narrow range of specific characteristics. And to that extent the possible specific characteristics of a simple quality are not totally dependent on their common generic characteristic but in fact, as a class, constitute a necessary condition of the latter. An instance of red need not be an instance of the specific shade of red which the color of region 1 is. But it must be an instance of *some* one specific shade in the range of shades which are red. It cannot be an instance of red unless it is an instance either of this shade of red, or that shade of red, or that other shade of red, etc. To the extent to which this is so, the noncommon, specific characteristics of two specifically different qualities are essential to their being what they are, and to that extent the identity of such qualities remains only generic and not specific.

The classical example of generic identity is that of an equilateral and an isosceles triangle. Both are figures enclosed by three lines. But they differ in respect to the proportions of the lengths of their three sides. Both characteristics, being a figure enclosed by three lines and being equilateral (or isosceles), are essential to *what* an equilateral triangle (or an isosceles triangle) is. An equilateral triangle which is not a figure enclosed by three lines is not an equilateral triangle at all. But neither is it equilateral if its three sides are not equal. To the extent to which the characteristic of equilateral triangularity, which an equilateral triangle does not have in common with an isosceles triangle, is essential to its being the triangle it is, the two triangles cannot be said to be identical. Yet there is a sense in which such noncommon characteristics can be regarded as logically secondary to the common characteristics, and thus, in a certain sense, as "accidental." An equilateral triangle is what it is only because it is a figure enclosed by three lines. Its characteristic of having three equal sides can be understood only by reference to the characteristic of being a figure enclosed by three lines; the former characteristic is not logically distinct from the latter, but constitutes a natural specification of the latter. On the other hand, the characteristic of being a figure enclosed by three lines need not be understood by reference to the characteristic of having three equal sides, it does not have to be specified in its instances in this particular way and not in some other way. To the extent to which this is the case, the noncommon characteristics of an equilateral and an isosceles triangle can be regarded as in a sense accidental to them, and the two qualities can be regarded as identical. At the same time, however, while an instance of being a figure enclosed by three lines need not be an instance of equilateral triangularity, it must be an instance of *some* one of the logically possible species of being a figure enclosed by three lines, i.e., the lengths of its three sides must be proportioned in one of the several ways which alone are logically possible. It cannot be an instance of triangularity unless it is an instance either of equilateral or isosceles or scalene triangularity. To the extent to which this is so, the noncommon characteristics of an equilateral triangle and an isosceles triangle are essential to their being the qualities they are and thus their identity remains only generic and not specific.

It is fashionable to classify inquiries into the relationship between the generic and specific characteristics of a quality either as disguised, and usually misleading and inaccurate, reports of the uses of certain words, e.g., color-adjectives and geometrical terms, or as useless, uninformative proposals of modifications in the uses of such words. For instance, it may be held that in saying that the possession of the characteristic of being pink entails the possession of the characteristic of being red, we are merely reporting a certain fact about the rules governing the uses of the words "pink" and "red." But such a view is quite misleading. Following the argument of Chapter Two, we must remember that words are not used in a vacuum; that their uses essentially reflect the nature of the concrete situations in which they occur and the nature of the objects which constitute such situations; and that to describe the use of a certain descriptive expression is to describe certain situations and objects in the world. Instead of saying that in stating that whatever is pink is also red we are merely stating that the rules of use of the words "pink" and "red" require us to predicate "red" of everything of which we predicate "pink," it is much more intelligible and much closer to the truth to say that in stating that the rules of use of the words "pink" and "red" require us to predicate "red" of everything of which we predicate "pink" we are really stating that it is a necessary fact about the world that everything pink is also red. Can we not notice this fact even if "pink" and "red" (or equivalent words) do not happen to be in our vocabulary?

16. The Observability
of Generic Universals

If two qualities which are generically identical in the sense I have just explained are observable elements of the world, then, to the extent to which their relationship is like literal identity, their identity and the generic universal which is its ground would also be observable.

As we have seen, the generic identity of two qualities depends on a certain logical relationship between their specific characteristics, which are not common, and their generic characteristic, which they have in common. The possession of the specific characteristic entails the possession of the generic characteristic, and the possession of the generic characteristic entails the possession of one and only one of many specific characteristics such that the possession of one of them entails the possession of that generic characteristic. Only if the noncommon, specific characteristics of two generically identical qualities are related to their common, generic characteristic in this way can one regard the qualities as identical without asserting that the specific and the generic characteristics of a quality are distinct components of the quality. It is this logical relationship alone that seems capable of meeting in a nonparadoxical manner the requirement that the generic universal which is the ground of the identity of two qualities be in a sense identical with, but in a sense also different from, the specific universals which are the ground of the qualitative difference between the two qualities. For the logical relationship I have described is such that the generic characteristic and the specific characteristic of a quality cannot be regarded as logically independent of one another; the possession of the one and the possession of the other are not logically distinct matters of fact. A logically necessary condition of the possession of the specific characteristic is the possession of the generic characteristic, and a logically necessary condition of the possession of the generic characteristic is the possession of one and only one of a certain determinate range of specific characteristics. It is not surprising, therefore, that the generic characteristic and the specific characteristic in a certain simple quality are not distinct components, as the shape and color of a color-patch or as even the sourness and sweetness of a taste seem to be. There is a fairly clear sense in which the generic and the specific characteristics are one and the same characteristic. At the same time, however, their sameness or identity is not literal. It would have been literal if, in addition to the fact that the possession of the specific characteristic entails the possession of the generic characteristic, it were also true that the possession of the generic characteristic entails the possession of the specific characteristic. And, to the extent to which this is not true, the generic and specific characteristics are not identical. But something *like* this is true. While the possession of the generic characteristic does not entail the possession of the specific characteristic, it does entail the possession of one of a certain range of such specific characteristics, the possession of each one of which would entail the possession of the generic characteristic. And this is why, while the specific and generic characteristics are not literally identical, their relationship is analogous to identity.

Now, if two generically identical qualities are observable, their specific characteristics must also be observable. As we have seen,[15] the specific characteristic of a simple quality is nothing but the simple quality itself. For the specific characteristic is the specific universal whose instance the quality is. And, assuming the truth of the claim of the Identity Theory that the location of a quality is not essential to the quality's being what it is, a quality is identical with the specific universal whose instance it is. But, assuming also that the above account of generic identity is correct, there is a sense in which

15. See p. 160.

the generic universal, which is the ground of the identity
of two inexactly resembling qualities, can be said to be
identical with the specific universals, which are the
ground of the difference between the two qualities.
And if the specific universals are observable (because
their instances are observable), then there is a corresponding sense in which the generic universal can also
be said to be observable. But it would be observable
only in a sense. For the identity of the generic universal
and the specific universals is not literal identity, it is
only very like literal identity. If it had been literal
identity, the generic universal would have been literally
observable; but then the qualities themselves would
have been specifically, and not merely generically, identical. As it is, the generic universal is observable only in
a sense, only with important qualifications, namely, the
qualifications which are parallel to the qualifications
that must be added to the statement that the two qualitatively different qualities are identical and to the qualifications that also must be added to the statement that
the generic universal is identical with the specific universals. At the same time, these necessary qualifications
should not be exaggerated by claiming that there is no
identity which is merely generic, that there is no sense
in which the specific and the generic characteristics of a
quality can be said to be identical, that either there are
not generic universals or generic universals are unobservable. The conditions of generic identity describe
a certain kind of fact about qualities, including the fact
that the specific and generic characteristics of each quality are related in a certain way. That there is such a fact
cannot be doubted. One can only refuse to classify it as

identity. My thesis has been that such a refusal would be mistaken for two reasons. First, the only alternative classification of this fact, namely, as a relation of resemblance, has been found to be unintelligible. Second, and this is an even more important reason, we have found fundamental similarities between this kind of fact about qualities and the kind of fact which is ordinarily described as the identity of an individual. The fact about the color of region 1 and the color of region 3, with the description of which we have been concerned in this chapter is, surely, much more like identity than it is like anything else. To refuse to classify it, with appropriate qualifications, as identity would be to deny ourselves an important insight into the nature of the world.

Even writers who would seem to agree, in general, with the above account of the genus-species relation fall into a peculiar error on the question of the observability and reality of generic universals. According to Professor Blanshard, ". . . the universal triangle or man or colour is not as such real. There is no abstract triangle or triangularity existing in all triangles as a little hard nucleus unaffected by the mode of its realization; there is no abstract humanity that is quite identical in all men; there is no colour that is colour in general. The generic universal lies not in the reality thought about, but in our thought about that reality." [16] The truth in this argument is that the generic universal is not an abstract universal, that it is not a distinct component of its instances, that it is not a specific universal. But this does not imply that it is not in the reality thought about but only in our thought about that reality. It should seem a

16. *Nature of Thought*, Vol. I, p. 652.

tautology that a genus can only be in its species, if it is anywhere. But its species are nothing but their instances considered identical. Consequently, it would seem that the genus must be in its instances. Why is it that Professor Blanshard denies this? Apart from certain general philosophical reasons which are peculiar to his philosophy, his reason is, I think, that he denies that the generic universal can be "unaffected by the mode of its realization" in its species. H. W. B. Joseph concurs with this denial. "So intimately one are the differentia and the genus, that though we refer different species to the same genus, yet the genus is not quite the same in each; it is only by abstraction, by ignoring their differences, that we can call it the same." [17] Here Joseph ignores the very point which he makes so persuasively elsewhere, namely, that the genus is that which is naturally and necessarily developed in its species. The genus is not-the-same in its species in the sense that it is not a species at all, that it is not an abstract universal. But it is the same in its species in the sense that each one of its species is comprehensible only as a species of the same genus. To reject the identity of the genus in its species because of fears of the Theory of Abstract Universals is to make the genus-species relationship unintelligible. It would be to confuse the genus with its species. The genus *is* in its species, and it is quite the same in all of its species. But, of course, it is in its species as a genus and not as a species. And to the extent to which it is identical with its species, it is as real and as observable as they are, and, thus, as their instances are.

17. *Introduction to Logic*, p. 83.

Conclusion

17. Summary. Concrete Universals.
  Universals as Causes.

I defined the subject of this inquiry as the question of
the proper description of the recurrence of qualities.
The Nominalist claim that the recurrence of a quality
consists merely in the fact that a certain general word is
in use, i.e., that a certain word applies to an indefinite
number of objects, was found to be quite unsatisfactory;
the recurrence of a quality is clearly a fact quite independent of language and only unsound arguments have
made it appear that it is not. We were left with a choice,
then, between identity and resemblance as the proper
classification of qualitative recurrence. It was tempting
to suppose that a preference for either one could merely
reflect linguistic custom or a somewhat confused desire
for violating such a custom. But we have found that
such a temptation must be resisted. Although the classification of recurrence is not a matter of experimental
discovery, it is not cognitively arbitrary. It constitutes
the assertion of an analogy between the fact of recur-

rence and other most general kinds of fact in the world. And such an analogy can be appropriate or inappropriate, illuminating or misleading, faithful to the nature of the world or distorting. We examined the Resemblance Theory and rejected it on the ground that its main claim, namely, that the recurrence of qualities is more like a relation of several distinct individual things, rather than like the identity of a single individual thing through time, is false. This conclusion, however, is not equivalent to the espousal of the Identity Theory. Indeed, the latter seems quite satisfactory with respect to specific identity. But in the case of generic identity it is faced with a major difficulty, which has usually constituted the reason for the rejection of the Identity Theory. A generic universal, it would seem, may only be unobservable. This already is disturbing to the empiricist. But, what is more important, it renders the very notion of generic identity absurd. For how can observable qualities of individual things, e.g., the color of A and the color of B, be unobservably identical, even if only generically? We have found, however, that the quick assumption that a generic universal may only be unobservable rests on an insufficiently examined conception of the connection between specific and generic universals. There is a peculiar logical relationship between a genus and its species, which in some important respects is like identity, although in other, also important, respects it is not like identity. To the extent to which it is like identity, it becomes quite proper to say that the generic universal is observable in its specific instances; to the extent to which it is not like identity, however, one could not say this. But *which* is it? Our conclusion should be that there are excellent reasons for making either claim and thus that one cannot say clearly and unequivocally that generic universals are observable. Nevertheless, the very fact that there is an intimate logical connection between a generic universal and its specific universals, one that is more like identity than like anything else even though it clearly is not literal identity, suggests that the gulf between the two is not as great as has been supposed. And, given the obvious fact that specific universals are observable, this should make generic universals much less mysterious and much more acceptable to the empiricist.

Our conclusion that the Identity Theory ought to be accepted, though with important reservations, is precisely the sort of thesis that encourages philosophers to build upon it sweeping theories about the nature of meaning and of thought, and about realms of being and levels of knowledge. There is ample historical evidence that such philosophical enterprises are involved in great danger. One such danger is that the philosopher may ignore the fact that, although the Identity Theory is quite relevant to such philosophical problems, their solutions depend on many other considerations and thus require separate and detailed investigations. This seems quite obvious in the case of the theory of meaning and the philosophy of mind. In fact, I doubt that these two branches of philosophy would profit very greatly from any theory of universals, although respect for the concept of universal and for the Identity Theory, which I have tried to justify in this essay, should have a beneficial influence on discussions that rather uncritically refuse to avail themselves of such helpful notions as property of an object and intension of a term. Our conclusions do seem to justify, in a very general way, the view that one can think of universals, both specific and generic, *qua* universals, regardless of whether such thought would employ images (if universals are observable, they are also imaginable), concepts, or words; as well as the view that certain words, namely, general and abstract singular terms, owe their meaningfulness in part to their association with universals. At least the empiricist should no longer object to these views. But, surely, the difficulties of explaining the nature of thought (how do we employ, in thinking, images or concepts or words, and do we really employ anything at all?) and the nature of the meaningfulness of general and abstract singular terms (how are words "associated" with something in the world, be it universal or particular, and are they, need they be, so associated?) remain undiminished. We may be much more hopeful, I believe, about the relevance of our conclusions to the theory of *a priori* knowledge and the theory of necessary truth. If there are universals, our knowledge of their relations would appear to be *a priori,* and the propositions describing these relations, necessary. At the same time, the observability of universals, even if qualified, should render the possibility of such knowledge and of such propositions much less mysterious. But, again, before any firm conclusions about these matters are reached, an account of the *very concepts* of *a priori* knowledge and of necessary truth must be given. And I see no particular contribution that any theory of universals can make to such an account.

The Identity Theory has usually been taken to have

several other, more direct, consequences. Two of them concern what perhaps are the most imposing theories proposed in the history of philosophy: the Platonic view that universals constitute a special realm of being which is entirely separate from the observable spatiotemporal world, and the Hegelian conception of the possibility of a deduction and *a priori* classification of concepts, as well as perhaps the deduction of the existence and nature of the world from the true and complete conceptual system. I shall call these two theories, respectively, the *Ante Rem* Theory of Universals and the Theory of Concrete Universals. The former will be the topic of the next and concluding section of this book. Here I shall consider briefly the version of the latter theory which connects it most clearly with the Identity Theory.[1]

In Chapter Four we recognized the intimate relationship between specific and generic universals, one very much like that of identity. The possession by an individual thing of a specific characteristic entails the possession of every one of the members of a hierarchical series of generic characteristics. And the possession of a generic characteristic entails the possession of one, and only one, of a certain determinate range of specific characteristics (and of subordinate generic characteristics, if any). The generic universal is thus, in a sense that I have dwelt on at length, identical with each of its species, and thus, in a corresponding sense, each of its species is identical with every other one. But then to have a con-

1. I make no attempt to reflect Hegel's (or Bradley's or Bosanquet's) views on the subject, but merely to draw attention to an interesting, though startling, possible consequence of the Identity Theory.

ception of a generic universal is to have, so to speak, all
of the conceptual material required for the conception
of each of its species. If we have an adequate conception
of the generic universal, we should be able to deduce
from it, purely *a priori,* the concepts of its species. And,
indeed, such a deduction is not wholly unfamiliar to us.
For instance, to conceive of the different kinds of triangle does not seem to require anything more than an
adequate conception of the nature of triangularity. The
conception of the characteristic of being a three-sided
figure would seem to contain everything necessary for,
nay, demand, force us to, the conception of the several
possible proportions of the sides of a triangle.

And corresponding to, though not the same as, the
genus-species relationship, there is the relationship of
the specific universal to its instances, which indeed is
quite like identity. The specific universal is identical
with each of its instances, and each of its instances is
identical with every other one. There is nothing in the
color of one part of a uniformly colored piece of paper
that is not in the color of any other part. Should it not
then be the case that to know the specific universal is
to know its instances, each one and all of them, and
everything about them, including their locations in
space and time?

Thus the universal is not abstract. It lives in its species
and instances, and they live in it. The generic universal
exists in and through its sub-genera and its species; the
specific universal exists in and through its instances. It
is appropriate to call such a universal concrete, one that
unites the moments of universality and particularity in
Reality, is identical with its species and its instances,

with all of them together and with each of them separately, and thus makes them the same in their diversity and diverse in their sameness. One might say that the universal, as concrete, is self-specifying and self-instantiating.

These are difficult views. Nevertheless, if my defense of the Identity Theory has been successful, they are not unfounded. They are also, I believe, of the greatest philosophical interest, in their own right. To reject them as obviously false would seem inexcusable. Our inability to understand the possibility of such deductions may be no more significant than would be an ignorant man's inability to understand the derivability of the remote theorems of plane geometry from its several definitions and axioms. In fact, are not such deductions of concepts of figures and numbers commonplace? And do we not perform some such deductions even of concepts of colors and sounds? Let us think of Hume's missing shade of blue. Nor may we dismiss the view (not held by Hegel) that Nature itself, in all of its particularity and detail, can be deduced from the Idea, on the ground that it ignores the special features of space and time. Such a conclusion would be philosophically respectable only on the basis of a respectable and thorough philosophy of space and time. Do we have such a philosophy?

At the same time, while the Theory of Concrete Universals should not be rejected on the basis of faith in realism, empiricism, and the scientific method, neither should it be accepted on the basis of conclusions from obscure theories about the role of thought in knowledge and of the spirit in reality. The impossibility of most of the deductions that ought to have been possible can hardly be explained by the limitations of our intelligence. And, more specifically, to the extent to which the theory derives all of its plausibility from the Identity Theory, we must remember that the latter is defensible only if it acknowledges (1) that generic identity is in no sense full-fledged, literal identity, and (2) that specific identity is possible only if the spatiotemporal location of an instance of a specific universal is in no way essential to that instance's being what it is. Should we be surprised then if we are unable to deduce either (1) concepts of specific universals from concepts of generic universals, or (2) spatiotemporal locations of instances of specific universals from concepts of specific universals? Perhaps the value of the Theory of Concrete Universals consists not so much in the truth of its belief in the possibility of an all-encompassing, purely *a priori* science as in the raising of the obviously important question, why should not such a science be possible?

The Theory of Concrete Universals could be regarded as the sophisticated, reasoned successor to the view (attributed by Aristotle to Plato, though with doubtful justification) that universals are the *causes* of the recurrences of qualities in the world, a view that, if taken literally, may only be described as fanciful. Indeed, if it means merely that if there were not universals then there would not be recurrences of qualities, it would be justified. For, as we have seen, the recurrence of qualities ought to be described as the presence, in a number of individual things, of one and the same universal quality. (And, for the same reason, it would also be true that things have their qualities, both "substantive" and "ac-

cidental," in virtue of the presence in them of universals; and that the causal roles of *things,* in so far as they
depend on the qualities that things have, depend on
the instantiation in things of certain universals, although such a causal role is not discoverable in the nature of the universal, nor is its reality guaranteed by the
existence of the universal.) But if the view in question
is taken to mean that a universal is the cause of its having been instantiated in certain individual things and
not in others or of its having been instantiated at all,
then it seems entirely unfounded and hardly intelligible, at least in so far as it is distinct from the Theory of
Concrete Universals.[2] While one who is acquainted
with the nature of triangularity is, *ipso facto,* acquainted
with the natures of the shape-qualities of all triangular
things, it does not follow that he is also acquainted with
the existence of any triangular things or with their other
characteristics that are not analytic consequences of
their being triangular, e.g., their aerodynamic properties. And, if we are to avoid confusing the problem of
universals with that of induction, we must also recognize that should we make inferences to unobserved
triangular things from what we have learned (by observation) about observed triangular things, e.g., their
aerodynamic properties, what might make such an in-

2. Plato assigned to the Demiurge that causal role, and the medi-
eval realists assigned it to God, although presumably without the
Forms or the Ideas in the Divine Mind such a causal role could not
have been performed. (A pastry form may be a standing, concomitant,
causal condition of the existence of certain pastries, but it is to the
cook, the principal cause, that we must appeal in an explanation of
the pastries' coming into being at a particular place and time, of their
number and distribution, and of the kinds of pieces of dough out of
which they have been made.)

ference possible would have nothing to do with the existence of the universal triangularity. All that the latter makes possible is the tautologous inference that if there are unobserved triangular things, then they are triangular (and also whatever being triangular entails). It does not even guarantee (nor in fact constitute the slightest reason for thinking) that there are unobserved triangular things at all.[3]

But even if there are nonspatiotemporal entities that cause the instantiation of universals, they should not be called universals at all. They would be more properly described as individuals with somewhat divine properties, each presiding over a certain recurrent quality and responsible for its presence in the world, e.g., a deity of the blueness in the world. Even if such an entity resembles the quality whose recurrence it has caused, the resemblance would not justify our regarding the entity as a universal, any more than the resemblance between a father (the "cause") and his sons (the "effects") would be a reason for regarding him as a universal, in any philosophically significant and useful sense of this term. A similar conclusion should be reached regarding the more complicated view that the entities in question (perhaps now thought of as the "patterns" of the things in the world) cause the recurrences of qualities only through the occasioning efficacy of a third entity, a Demiurge. A pastry form, no less than a father, is, in any useful philosophical terminology, an individual thing, not a universal, even though, when used by the cook, it produces in pieces of dough a recurrent, universal shape,

3. For a different approach to this issue, see Manley Thompson, "Abstract Entities and Universals," *Mind*, 1965.

or instantiates in them a universal shape that it itself, the pastry form, also instantiates. It should be observed that such views about the causal origin of the recurrences of qualities are compatible with all three theories of universals we have distinguished. The applicability of one and the same word to qualities of individual things, and the resemblance of these qualities, would be explainable, no less than their identity, by the causal efficacy of the Deities of Recurrent Qualities.

18. The Ante Rem Theory of Universals

While the view of universals as causes seems fanciful and the Theory of Concrete Universals implausible, their immediate relative, the *Ante Rem* Theory, is neither fanciful nor implausible. On the contrary, it draws attention to some extremely important facts about the relationship between individual things and their universal qualities, which any theory of universals must recognize and take into account.

Ordinarily, to say that an entity is spatiotemporal, that it is in space and in time, that it is "in the world," is to say that it has a *location* in space and in time, that it occupies a certain place and lasts through a certain period of time. Again, commonly, to say that an entity has a location in space and in time is to say that it has a *unique* location, that it can be assigned to only one geometrically continuous place and to only one continuous period of time. Clearly, in this sense, a universal quality has no location in space or in time and is not in space and in time. Is there another sense of "spatiotemporal location"? It would seem that there is. At least the rudiments of a notion of multiple spatiotemporal location can be found in ordinary discourse. Pakistan and the University of California can be said to be located at more than one place at the same time. Poland and some small colleges with unhappy histories can be said to have existed intermittently, during several non-contiguous periods of time. Indeed, the significance of such examples is doubtful. But they do suggest a way of establishing a notion of a multiply located entity that would bear at least some resemblance to a universal quality. We might wish to regard, for example, all red surfaces in the universe as constituting one single entity. Then we could give a clear sense to the term "multiple location" simply be stipulating that such an entity is located wherever and whenever a red surface is located. The Red Object would be located in many places at the same time and in many periods of time. But while there is no difficulty in introducing the notion of a multiply located entity in this manner, it should be clear that such an entity would bear only superficial similarity to a universal quality. A universal quality is not the collection of its instances but rather the pervasive qualitative nature of these instances. I have introduced the notion of universal quality in the context of the Identity Theory of the recurrence of qualities. And, in that context, to say that there are universal qualities is to say that certain qualities of distinct individual things are one and the same, identical quality, rather than distinct qualities related by a relation of resemblance. But the parts of an entity which has multiple spatiotemporal location are not identical, they do not constitute one entity in the sense that each one is the same as the other.

The major claim of the Identity Theory, which gives content to the notion of universal quality, is that the relationship between the instances of a recurrent quality is analogous to the identity of a man through time. But the relationship between the parts of a multiply located object is analogous to that of the arms, legs, trunk, and head of a man. This is why the multiply located Red Object can be divided into two halves, part of it can be annihilated, and it can be changed in all of the ways in which the surfaces which constitute it can be changed. But it would be nonsensical to say that the color red can be divided into two halves, that part of it can be annihilated, or that it changes whenever the surfaces of red things change.

In what sense, then, can a universal quality be said to be in space and in time, to be "in the world"? Clearly, only in the sense that the individual things in which it is instantiated have unique locations in space and in time, and are in the world. This is a sense very different from the sense in which tables, mesons, and horse races are said to be in space and in time. And perhaps the difference is so great that it would be important and enlightening to assert that universal qualities are not in space and time at all, that they are not in the world.

The qualitative *nature* of a universal quality is completely independent of changes in the existence, identity, characteristics, relations, and causal properties of the things in which it is instantiated. The destruction of a circular thing makes no difference to the geometrical properties of the circle. A blue book may be soaked in water, soiled, torn into pieces, glued to a red book, and even painted red. It would be nonsensical to say that such changes affect the qualitative nature of the color blue. But it is not only the qualitative nature of a universal quality that remains unaffected by changes in the existence, characteristics, and relations of the things in which it is instantiated—at least to some degree, so is its existence. Even if the annihilation of all blue things in the universe would also be the annihilation of the color blue, it seems obvious that the annihilation of any *particular* blue thing or any *particular* group of blue things is completely irrelevant to the existence of the color blue. The destruction of one half of all blue things in the universe would not make it less likely that there is such a color as blue, nor would it cause only one half of the color blue to exist, nor would it make the color blue somehow "semi-exist." Thus the fact that a universal quality has instances appears somewhat accidental and quite unimportant. If the existence of all but one of the instances of a universal quality is entirely irrelevant to the existence of the universal quality itself, why should the existence of that one instance, whichever it may be, *constitute* the existence of the universal quality? The natural conclusion of this train of thought is that a universal quality may exist even if it has no instances at all. And such a conclusion could also receive support from the fact that ordinarily we do assert the existence of universal qualities without paying any attention to the existence or nonexistence of their instances. We assert that there are five, and only five, regular polyhedrons, without at all intending to assert that in fact there are individual things which exemplify such shapes. A woman, engaged in planning

the decoration of her house, may say, with perfect intelligibility, "Of course, there is always orange that
could go well with the color of the draperies but there
might not be anything of the right shade." And an
architect may explain to his client, with equal intelligibility, that there are seven arrangements of the rooms
of a seven-room house, although two of them would be
so inconvenient that probably they have never been
tried.

Nevertheless, the conclusion that a universal quality
may exist even if it has no instances is in need of further support. The appeal to ordinary discourse is de-
ceptive. What is of interest is not the fact that we do
assert the existence of universal qualities without paying any attention to the existence or nonexistence of
their instances (has anyone doubted that we do?), but
the *sense* of such assertions. For, the use of the term
"existence" with respect to such qualities might be
purely idiomatic, or it might be a sign of an ordinary
ambiguity in its meaning; and then its philosophical
significance would be no greater than the sociological
significance of the fact that some bachelors (of arts) are
married. If the applicability of the notion of existence
to uninstantiated universal qualities is to be explained,
a clear and usable criterion for such an application must
be stated. And if it is to be shown to be philosophically
interesting, there must be shown significant similarities
between this criterion and the criteria for the paradigmatic uses of the term "existence," in order that the
classification of the former as a criterion of *existence*
would be important. The strength of the defender of

the existence of uninstantiated universal qualities is due mainly to his ability to provide such a criterion and to show that there are such similarities.[4]

There is at least one clear and usable criterion of the existence of a universal quality that may not have instances, namely, the logical possibility that an individual thing should have that quality. In virtue of the very notion of quality, if there is a certain quality then it must be logically possible for some individual thing to have that quality. And if there are any reasons at all for asserting the existence of a universal quality that may not have instances, surely the logical possibility that something has that quality would constitute such a reason. To deny that the existence of a universal quality entails the logical possibility of the instantiation of that universal quality would be to make the notion of quality incoherent. And a denial that the logical possibility of the instantiation of a universal quality entails the existence of the universal quality can only be motivated by a refusal to allow for any criterion of the existence of uninstantiated qualities, and not

---

4. Consider the following analogy. It is an important fact about the nature of government that a government may exist even if it has lost the greater part of the territory and population over which it had control. For this fact suggests the possibility of an application of the notion of government even to bodies which have no control over any territory and population. And, in fact, we sometimes do apply this notion to such bodies, e.g., to governments-in-exile. But if one is to explain this application of the notion of government one must state a clear and usable criterion for it (how do we distinguish between a government-in-exile and an ordinary organization of exiles?). And if one is to demonstrate its importance to our understanding of the nature of government, one must show that there are significant similarities between this criterion and the criteria for the paradigmatic applications of the notion of government (e.g., in both cases a kind of recognition by other governments might be required).

by dissatisfaction with this particular criterion. Thus the necessary and sufficient condition of the truth of the architect's statement that there is a certain way of arranging the rooms of the seven-room house, though it may never have been tried, is that it is logically possible for a seven-room house to have its rooms so arranged. And the necessary and sufficient condition of the truth of the woman's assertion of the existence of a certain shade of orange is that it is logically possible for something to be of such a shade. Indeed, there is a certain ambiguity in the statement of the criterion, due to the distinction between logical and real possibility, which is not clearly made in ordinary thought and discourse. But this ambiguity, though worthy of investigation, does not affect the fact that the criterion is, in general, a clear and usable one, and that it is quite capable of supporting assertions of the existence of uninstantiated qualities. It is also true that a complete account of it must include a theory of the nature of logical possibility. But for the purposes of demonstrating that there is such a criterion, it is not necessary to presuppose any particular account of logical possibility. One may determine that it is logically possible for something to have a certain quality by appealing to the rules of language, or by imagining something that has that quality, or by noting that there is no formal contradiction in the proposition that there exists something which has that quality, etc.

But is the above criterion our only criterion of the existence of an uninstantiated quality? Two other criteria may be proposed. First, it may be claimed that the necessary and sufficient condition of the existence of such a quality is that it can be an object of intellectual

intuition, of a special kind of nonsensory, purely spirit-
ual awareness. Now let us allow that there can be such
a kind of awareness, and that it can be the source of our
knowledge of the existence of certain entities. But, as
we have noted before, if such an entity is to be classifiable as a universal, in any distinctive, useful sense of
this technical term, it must at least be *capable* of *being*
the qualities of several distinct individual things at the
same time. Otherwise, it would be merely a very peculiar
individual entity, the application to which of the notion of universal would mean nothing and only breed
confusion. But, now, if the qualities of distinct individual things which the universal quality is at least
capable of *being* would be observable, the supposition
that the universal quality itself is unobservable, and
that moreover it is an object of a special nonsensory and
purely intellectual kind of awareness, becomes thoroughly unintelligible.[5] On the other hand, if the qualities of the individual things would themselves be unobservable, if they too are objects of intellectual intuition, then indeed the universal quality too would be
such an object. But in that case the proposed criterion
would be applicable only to the universal qualities of
unobservable, intelligible individual entities (e.g., angels), or to universal qualities the instances of which
are unobservable, intelligible qualities of observable
individual things (if such a combination is possible).
And even then there would be the probably insuperable
difficulty of giving sense to the distinction between being intellectually aware of an uninstantiated universal

5. Cf. above, section 13.

quality and being intellectually aware of an instance of that quality.[6] Second, it may also be claimed that the necessary and sufficient condition of the existence of an uninstantiated universal quality is that one can think of such a quality. But the phrase "thinking of a quality" is ambiguous. If to say that one is thinking of an uninstantiated universal quality is to say that one is actually *aware* of that quality, then this criterion collapses into the one from intellectual intuition. If to think of such a quality is to contemplate a mental image, or to think in some non-imaginative manner, of an individual *thing* that has that quality, then the proposed criterion seems to be merely a special version of the criterion from logical possibility, required by the espousal of a particular theory of the nature of logical possibility. And, finally, if to think of a universal quality is to contemplate a mental image which actually contains an instance of the universal quality (e.g., a mental image of a red tomato which is itself red), then the proposed criterion is no longer a criterion for the existence of *uninstantiated* universal qualities; and also it is based on the difficult assumption that an image of a red tomato, although it cannot itself be a tomato, can nevertheless itself be red.[7]

6. Cf. the scholastic doctrine that the angels, if they are to be distinguishable at all, must each be the sole member of a distinct species.

7. It has also been suggested (by Manley Thompson, "Abstract Entities," *Philosophical Review*, 1960) that "for an abstract entity to be is to be a member of a logical system" (p. 346), that "a color exists when it has a place in a system of colors" (p. 345). But a system *of* what? Presumably, of abstract entities, e.g., of colors. And thus the proposed criterion would be like saying that for a spatiotemporal entity to be is to be a member of the system of spatiotemporal entities. But Thompson's dictum may be true if it is intended not as a *general*

However, as we have seen, it is not enough that a clear and usable criterion of the existence of uninstantiated universal qualities be stated. If this criterion is to be usefully classifiable as a criterion of *existence,* if it is not to be the mere source of an ordinary ambiguity in the meaning of the word "existence," if it is to be philosophically interesting, one must also show that there are important similarities between it and the criteria for the paradigmatic uses of the term "existence." Now it seems obvious that the paradigm of the notion of existence is the existence of an individual thing. It must be shown, therefore, that there are important similarities between the existence of individual things and the logical possibility of the instantiation of universal qualities. Indeed, there are such similarities, and a reference to them completes the case for the *Ante Rem* Theory. Just as the existence of an individual thing (e.g., a rabbit in the woods) is not a matter of caprice, personal preference, or wishful thinking, so is the logical possibility of the instantiation of a universal quality (e.g., a certain way of arranging the rooms of a house). Just as there are rules and strategies for determining the existence of an individual thing, so are there rules and strategies for determining the logical possibility of the instantiation of a universal quality. Both are objects of *discovery.* Both are, so to speak, hard facts with which we may be confronted and which we may study, and to which we must adjust our actions and beliefs.

criterion of the existence of an abstract entity, but as an observation to the effect that we think of abstract entities as members of systems, and that we often determine that there is a certain abstract entity on the basis of the fact that there are certain other, related abstract entities.

And the role of questions concerning the logical possibility of instances of universal qualities in our thought and discourse about universal qualities is quite similar to the role of questions concerning the existence of individual things in our thought and discourse about individual things. Just as there is an obvious distinction between asking whether an individual thing exists and asking for a description of it, so is there a distinction between asking whether it is possible for something to have a certain universal quality and asking for a description of the characteristics and relations of that quality. Just as the supposition of the existence of a certain individual thing is a necessary condition of the description of its characteristics, so the supposition of the logical possibility of an instance of a universal quality (e.g., a twenty-sided regular polyhedron) is a necessary condition of the description of its characteristics. The determination of the existence of individual things constitutes the foundations of our knowledge of individual things. The determination of the logical possibility of the instantiation of universal qualities constitutes the foundations of our knowledge of universal qualities. And the greater familiarity of the notion of existence, due probably to the fact that we are much more interested in the existence of individual things than in the logical possibility of instances of universal qualities, makes quite natural the introduction of a sense of "existence" such that to say that a universal quality exists is to say that it is logically possible for an individual thing to have that quality.

It is with considerations such as these that the *Ante Rem* Theory could support its claim that there is a realm of being quite distinct and separate from the observable, spatiotemporal world. Clearly, there is nothing fanciful about this claim. Behind it stands the recognition of extremely important facts about the relationship between individual things and universal qualities. To argue that it is obviously false would be absurd. The notions of spatiotemporal entity and of existence are so complex and their boundaries so indeterminate that such a rejection of the *Ante Rem* Theory would be scandalous. The differences between individual things and their universal qualities are fundamental and far-reaching. It would hardly be surprising that the criteria for the application of the notion of existence to universal qualities should be different from the criteria for its application to individual things, and that the notion of being in space and time should be applicable only to individual things. Indeed, the claim of the *Ante Rem* Theory, though backed by excellent reasons, may still have fatal defects. Or it may be a case of unjustified exaggeration of the importance of certain facts. But whether this is so can be determined with finality only on the basis of a thorough, full-scale examination of the notions of space, time, and existence. Philosophical problems are neither solved nor clarified with accusations of "platonic mystification," proclamations of loyalty to "empiricism," or declarations of disbelief in "abstract entities."

On the other hand, our tolerance with the *Ante Rem* Theory must be intelligent. The denial of the existence of universal qualities in space and time must not be interpreted as lending support to the view that such qualities are not really the qualities of individual things in the spatiotemporal world, that they are literally separate from their instances, that since they have neither unique nor multiple locations in the spatiotemporal world they are "somewhere else." Were this view accepted, the notion of universal quality would become forthwith unintelligible and thus the *Ante Rem* Theory of universals would lose its only possible basis: the acceptance of the Identity Theory of the recurrence of qualities. There may be all sorts of nonspatiotemporal entities. But such an entity can usefully be classified also as a universal only if it can be "shared in" by distinct individual things, only if it can be a characteristic of more than one individual thing at the same time. If there are nonspatiotemporal individual things, then their qualities may be universals which have no connection with the spatiotemporal world. What is not possible, however, is that the qualities of spatiotemporal individual things are such universals.

Nor should the assertion of the existence of uninstantiated universal qualities be interpreted in such a way that the sense in which universal qualities can be said to exist without instances would appear to be at all the same as the sense in which stars without planets are said to exist. Were it given such an interpretation, its proponent would be led irresistibly to the view that universal *qualities* are a special kind of *individual* entities, entirely separate from and logically independent of the individual things with which they may or may not enter in the relation of instantiation. And this view is thoroughly unintelligible, for it renders the very notions of universal quality and instantiation vacuous. There are crucial, absolutely fundamental differences between the criteria for the application of the notion of existence to individual things, such as stars without planets, and the criteria for its application to universal qualities without instances, despite the analogy between them to which the *Ante Rem* Theory has usefully drawn attention. The criterion for asserting the existence of a universal quality without instances is the logical possibility of there being an individual thing that has that quality. And, as we have seen, there should be no doubt that this is our *only* criterion for asserting the existence of a universal quality without instances. But the criteria for asserting the existence of stars without planets are strikingly, obviously different, however difficult it may be to state them. There are ways of identifying a star and reasons for asserting its existence that have nothing to do with the existence of its planets or with the possibility that it may have planets. And it would be absurd to assert the existence of a certain star solely on the grounds that it is logically possible for some planet to have it as its star. Nor is it a curious accident that the logical possibility of there being an individual thing that has a certain universal quality should be our one and only criterion for asserting the existence of that universal quality. On the contrary, it is a direct consequence of the fact that the notion of universal is intelligible and its introduction serves a distinct philosophical function only as a means of describing the fact of the recurrence of the qualities of individual things.

It would be useless to argue that, since to say that it is logically possible for an individual thing to have a certain universal quality is to say that the universal quality is *potentially* the quality of an individual thing, it follows that the uninstantiated universal quality must *actually* be something else. To argue in this way for the existence of a literally separate realm of universals would be to apply to qualities the distinction between potentiality and actuality as it is applied to individual things (e.g., something is potentially a house but actually must be something else, perhaps timber). And to do so would be to ignore precisely the fundamental differences between individual things and their qualities which originally made the *Ante Rem* Theory plausible and thus, indirectly, rendered the application of the notion of existence to uninstantiated universal qualities possible. An individual thing becomes actually what it had been only potentially by ceasing to have some qualities and acquiring new qualities. To suppose that its qualities themselves can go through such a process of actualization would be incoherent. A universal quality is not an individual thing. This is why it need not be actually something else if potentially it is the quality of an individual thing.

Bibliography

The following list consists primarily of contemporary books and articles referred to in the text. I have supplemented it with a few other works of closely related interest, in order to make the list more useful. Needless to say, many of the most important discussions of the problem of universals are to be found in Plato, Aristotle, Augustine, Boethius, Abelard, Albert the Great, Thomas Aquinas, Duns Scotus, William of Ockham, Spinoza, Locke, Berkeley, Hume, and Hegel. Bibliographical guidance to them is available in good histories of philosophy, such as Frederick Copleston's.

BOOKS

Aaron, R. I. *Our Knowledge of Universals.* London: Humphrey Milford, 1945. British Academy Annual Philosophical Lecture.
———. *The Theory of Universals.* Oxford: The Clarendon Press, 1952.
Austin, J. L. *Philosophical Papers.* Oxford: The Clarendon Press, 1961. See especially Chapters 1 and 2.
Ayer, A. J. *Philosophical Essays.* London: Macmillan and Co. Ltd., 1954. See especially Chapters 1, 2, 5, and 9.
Bergmann, Gustav. *Meaning and Existence.* Madison: University of Wisconsin Press, 1960.

————. *Logic and Reality*. Madison: University of Wisconsin Press, 1964.

Blanshard, Brand. *The Nature of Thought*. 2 vols. London: George Allen and Unwin Ltd., 1939. See especially Chapters XVI and XVII.

Bochenski, I. M., Alonzo Church, and Nelson Goodman. *The Problem of Universals*. Notre Dame: University of Notre Dame Press, 1956.

Bosanquet, Bernard. *The Principle of Individuality and Value*. London: Macmillan and Co. Ltd., 1927. See especially Lecture II.

Bradley, F. H. *The Principles of Logic*. 2d ed., 2 vols. London: Oxford University Press, 1922. See especially Chapter VI.

Church, R. W. *An Essay on Critical Appreciation*. Ithaca: Cornell University Press, 1938. See especially Chapter 1.

————. *An Analysis of Resemblance*. London: Allen and Unwin, 1952.

Goodman, Nelson. *The Structure of Appearance*. Cambridge: Harvard University Press, 1951.

Hampshire, Stuart. *Thought and Action*. London: Chatto and Windus, 1960. See especially Chapter 1.

Joseph, H. W. B. *Introduction to Logic*. 2d ed. rev. Oxford: The Clarendon Press, 1916. See especially Chapters 2, 3, 4, 5, and 6.

Johnson, W. E. *Logic*. 3 vols. Cambridge: The University Press, 1921. See especially Vol. I, Part I, Chapters VII, VIII, IX, and XI.

Moore, G. E. *Some Main Problems of Philosophy*. London: George Allen and Unwin Ltd., 1953. See especially Chapters XVI-XX.

Price, H. H. *Thinking and Representation*. London: G. Cumberlege, 1946. British Academy Annual Philosophical Lecture.

————. *Thinking and Experience*. London: Hutchinson's University Library, 1953. See especially Chapter I.

Quine, W. V. O. *From a Logical Point of View*. 2d ed. rev. Cambridge: Harvard University Press, 1961.

————. *Word and Object*. Cambridge: The Technology Press of Massachusetts Institute of Technology, 1960. See especially Chapter 7.

Ramsey, F. P. *The Foundations of Mathematics*. London: Routledge and Kegan Paul Ltd., 1931. See especially Chapters IV, V, and VI.

Russell, Bertrand. *The Problems of Philosophy*. London: G. Cumberlege, 1950. See especially Chapters IX and X.

Shwayder, D. S. *Modes of Referring and the Problem of Universals*. Berkeley and Los Angeles: University of California Press, 1961.

Stout, G. F. *The Nature of Universals and Propositions*. London: Oxford University Press, 1921. British Academy Annual Philosophical Lecture.

Strawson, P. F. *Individuals*. London: Methuen and Co. Ltd., 1959. See especially Part II.

Wilson, John Cook. *Statement and Inference*. 2 vols. Oxford: The Clarendon Press, 1926. See especially Vol. I, Part II, Chapters XV-XVIII, and Vol. II, Part V.

ARTICLES

Aaron, R. I. "Two Senses of the Word *Universal*," *Mind*, XLVIII (1939): 168-185.

Acton, H. B. "The Theory of Concrete Universals I," *Mind*, XLV (1936): 417-431.

———. "The Theory of Concrete Universals II," *Mind*, XLVI (1937): 1-13.

Bambrough, J. R. "Universals and Family Resemblances," *Proceedings of the Aristotelian Society*, LXI (1961): 207-223.

Brandt, Richard B. "The Languages of Realism and Nominalism," *Philosophy and Phenomenological Research*, XVII (1957): 516-536.

Ducasse, C. J. "Some Critical Comments on a Nominalistic Analysis of Resemblance," *Philosophical Review*, 49 (1940): 641-648.

Foster, M. B. "The Concrete Universal: Cook Wilson and Bosanquet," *Mind*, XL (1931): 1-22.

Goodman, Nelson, and W. V. O. Quine. "Steps toward a Constructive Nominalism," *Journal of Symbolic Logic*, XII (1947): 105-123.

Hampshire, Stuart. "Scepticism and Meaning," *Philosophy*, XXV
  (1950): 235-246.
Jones, J. R. "Are the Qualities of Particular Things Universal
  or Particular?," *Philosophical Review*, LVIII (1949): 152-170.
————. "Characters and Resemblances," *Philosophical Review*,
  LX (1951): 551-562.
Klemke, E. D. "Universals and Particulars in a Phenomenalist
  Ontology," *Philosophy of Science*, XXVII (1960): 254-261.
Lazerowitz, M. "The Existence of Universals," *Mind*, LV (1946):
  1-24.
Moore, G. E. "Are the Characteristics of Particular Things Uni-
  versal or Particular?," *Proceedings of the Aristotelian Society*,
  Supp. III, 1923, pp. 95-113. Reprinted in *Philosophical Papers*,
  London: George Allen and Unwin Ltd., 1959.
O'Connor, D. J. "On Resemblance," *Proceedings of the Aristo-
  telian Society*, XLVI (1945-46): 47-77.
Pap, Arthur. "Nominalism, Empiricism, and Universals I," *Philo-
  sophical Quarterly*, 9 (1959): 330-340.
————. "Nominalism, Empiricism, and Universals II," *Philo-
  sophical Quarterly*, 10 (1960): 44-60.
Pears, D. "Universals," *Philosophical Quarterly*, 1 (1950-51): 218-
  227.
Prior, A. N. "Determinables, Determinates, and Determinants,"
  I and II, *Mind*, LVIII (1949): 1-20 and 178-194.
Quinton, A. "Properties and Classes," *Proceedings of the Aris-
  totelian Society*, LVIII (1957-58): 33-58.
Raphael, D. Daiches. "Universals, Resemblance, and Identity,"
  Proceedings of the Aristotelian Society, LV (1954-55): 109-133.
Russell, Bertrand. "On the Relations of Universals and Particu-
  lars," *Proceedings of the Aristotelian Society*, XII (1911-12):
  1-25.
Searle, J. "On Determinables and the Notion of Resemblance,"
  The Aristotelian Society, Supp. Vol. XXXIII, 1959, pp. 141-159.
Sellars, Wilfrid. "Grammar and Existence: A Preface to On-
  tology," *Mind*, LXIX (1960): 499-533.
————. "Abstract Entities," *Review of Metaphysics*, XVI (1963):
  627-671.

Smith, Norman Kemp. "The Nature of Universals," I, II, and III, *Mind*, XXXVI (1927): 137-157, 265-280, and 393-422.

Stout, G. F. "Are the Characteristics of Particular Things Universal or Particular?," *Proceedings of the Aristotelian Society*, Supp. Vol. III, 1923, pp. 114-122.

Strawson, P. F. "On Particular and General," *Proceedings of the Aristotelian Society*, LIV (1953-54): 233-261.

Thompson, Manley. "Abstract Terms," *Philosophical Review*, LXVIII (1959): 281-302.

————. "Abstract Entities," *Philosophical Review*, LXIX (1960): 331-350.

————. "Abstract Entities and Universals," *Mind*, LXXIV (1965): 365-382.

Urmson, J. O. "Recognition," *Proceedings of the Aristotelian Society*, LVI (1955-56): 259-281.

Wolterstorff, Nicholas. "Qualities," *Philosophical Review*, LXIX (1960): 183-200.

Index